Prayers to Share

Year A

Dedication

This book is dedicated to the church members and friends who, through all the Sundays of the church year, have shared prayers with me. We have offered prayers to God at

Ipswich Road United Reformed Church, Norwich, England
Lakenham United Reformed Church, Norwich, England
Princes Street United Reformed Church, Norwich, England
Knox United Church (Pruden Street), Thunder Bay, Canada
First Church United, Thunder Bay, Canada
St. Andrew's United Church, Schreiber, Canada
Terrace Bay Community Church, Terrace Bay, Canada
Westminster United Church, Thunder Bay, Canada
Duff United Church, Duff, Canada
Grace United Church, Lemberg, Canada
Knox United Church, Abernethy, Canada
St. Andrew's United Church, Balcarres, Canada

David Sparks

PRAYERS TO SHARE YEAR A

Responsive Prayers for each Sunday of the Church Year

Revised Common Lectionary based

WOOD LAKE BOOKS

Editors: Heather Picotte and Michael Schwartzentruber
Cover and interior design: Margaret Kyle

WOOD LAKE BOOKS, INC. acknowledges the financial support of the Government of Canada, through the Book Publishing Industry Development Program (BPIDP) for our publishing activities.

At Wood Lake Books we practice what we publish, guided by a concern for fairness, justice, and equal opportunity in all of our relationships with employees and customers.

We recycle and reuse and encourage readers to do the same. Resources are printed on recycled paper and more environmentally friendly groundwood papers (newsprint), whenever possible. The trees used are replaced through donations to the Scoutrees for Canada program. A percentage of all profit is donated to charitable organizations.

Library and Archives Canada Cataloguing in Publication

Sparks, David, 1938–

Prayers to share, year A: responsive prayers for each Sunday of the church year/David Sparks.

"Revised Common lectionary based".

Accompanied by a CD-ROM containing text of Prayers to share, years A–C.

Includes indexes.

ISBN 1-55145-507-2

1. Pastoral prayers. 2. Church year – Prayer-books and devotions – English. I. Title.

BV250.S6 2004 264'.13 C2004-904180-0

Published by
Wood Lake Books, Inc.
Kelowna, BC
www.woodlakebooks.com

Printing 10 9 8 7 6 5 4 3 2 1

Printed in Canada
by Transcontinental Printing

Contents

Preface

To pray, to give thanks and praise to God, who has given us everything and without whom we are nothing, is the most natural act in the world. To able to pray with other members of the faith community Sunday by Sunday is an awesome privilege. But what form should this public prayer take?

This is the final volume of *Prayers to Share,* which affirms that prayer in worship is not just a solo act of the minister, priest, or lay worship leader. Nor is it an unthinking chorus of leader and people together. It is, or should be, a dynamic, responsive act that captures the hearts and minds of congregational members and brings glory to God.

The *Revised Common Lectionary* provides a solid, scriptural basis for our prayers. Through the lectionary, the seasons of the church year are followed and the wide spectrum of the scriptures, Hebrew and Christian, is honoured. Many of the prayers in this book are derived from or inspired by the readings appointed for a particular week or season.

It is my hope that those of you who lead worship will be helped in different ways by the weekly set of prayers provided here. Some of you will find that my style fits well with your own style, and that you can use these prayers as they are printed. Some of you will want to change words or phrases so that you feel comfortable with them and so that the congregation can sense that the prayers are in tune with the situation of their faith community. And, no doubt, some of you will simply want to look at the prayer patterns and work out your own themes and words for a particular week. For example, in the "Confession" prayers, I have tended not to use the traditional "miserable offender" approach, but have offered affirmations, reminders, encouragement, and questions instead.

For years, the sermon has been considered by many to be the center of the worship experience. In my experience, it is certainly the thing most often commented on by people as they leave the worship service. I believe, however, that a worship service should be a thematic whole and that the prayers, hymns, sermon, music, and dramatic presentation should complement, reflect, and build on one another. Moreover, it is "liturgy" (the work of the people) that we are about. Worship leaders are responding faithfully when the congregation is engaged in worship, and what better way of engaging the congregation than through active, responsive participation in prayers throughout the service?

My thanks for so much support and help go out to the many different persons at Wood Lake Books who have been involved in the *Prayers to Share* project. I would mention especially the three editors, Mike Schwartzentruber, Jim Taylor, and Heather Picotte, who in their different ways have shaped the three volumes so creatively, and Margaret Kyle for her eye-pleasing design work.

Thanks also to my wife Kathy, a sustaining and loving presence in the testing times of writing and revising sets of prayers.

As I complete this task, I am acutely aware of the ways in which the members of the pastoral charges I have served have fed my prayer life. It is their joy, their challenges, their questions, their tough places, and their reflections on scripture that are mirrored in these pages. To them, and to the One All-Loving God, I offer my profound thanks.

Advent 1

Lectionary Readings
Isaiah 2:1-5
Psalm 122
Romans 13:11-14
Matthew 24:36-44

Call to Worship

One: Isaiah prophesies, "They will hammer their swords into ploughs." Christ is coming!

All: We await the coming of the One who brings peace.

One: Isaiah prophesies, "The people who walked in darkness have seen a great light."
Christ is coming!

All: We await the coming of the One who brings light to those who know darkness.

One: Isaiah prophesies, "A new king will arise from the descendants of David."
Christ is coming!

All: We await the coming of the One who brings justice and integrity. Christ is coming! Christ is coming! Rejoice, rejoice!

Opening Prayer

One: Loving God, speak to us gently at this Coming of Jesus time, for his presence touches our hearts;

All: tell us of his lowly birth in utter powerlessness, remind us of his healing touch for the distressed.

One: Speak to us gently;

All: bring to mind his heartening words to the poor, his comfort to those despised and rejected.

One: Speak to us gently;

All: recall for us the way Jesus weaves people together into faith community.

One: Speak to us gently;

All: bring home his message of hope for our own tough times.
One: Loving God, speak to us gently at this Coming of Jesus time,
All: and grant to us all, faithful listening. Amen.

Prayer of Confession

One: The Season of Advent is a time of reflection, confession, and prayer.
All: If we have been too busy to be still before you, O God, forgive us.
One: The Season of Advent is a time to consider our priorities.
**All: If we have given first place to getting and spending,
O God, forgive us.**
One: The Season of Advent is a time for giving from our abundance.
**All: If we have been reluctant to share time or money,
O God, forgive us.**
One: The Season of Advent is a time of reunion and reconciliation.
All: If we have neglected family members or friends, O God, forgive us.
One: The Season of Advent is the time to greet your Chosen One,
Jesus Christ.
**All: If we have neglected the story of your love, come humbly
to be with all people, O God, forgive us.**
Time of silence…

Words of Assurance

One: Give us the true meaning of this Advent season, O God.
**All: Deepen our prayerfulness;
alert us to the needs of the community;
enable us to give generously;
open our hearts with compassion;
remind us of Jesus, the One for whom we wait.**
One: In grace-filled waiting, God's peace will be yours, God's pardon
will be experienced.
All: Thanks be to God. Amen.

Offering Prayer

One: O God, accept this money offered, accept our gifts given, accept the good will of our hearts for those who will receive, so that:

All: disappointment may be replaced by joy;
worry may be replaced by happiness,
hopelessness may be replaced by a sense of purpose,
rejection may be replaced by acceptance,
and an ordinary meal may become a feast.

One: Bless all our gifts, for we await with wonder the birth of Jesus Christ.

All: Amen.

Commissioning

One: The joys and the hard places of the world await us,
but we have been fed with spiritual food.

All: We have been encouraged as a faith community;
we have been motivated to serve the powerless;
we have been challenged as those who own the name of Jesus Christ.
We leave with Advent hope in our hearts.

Advent 2

Alternatives here are offered for those worship leaders using "general Advent," and for those who stay with John the Baptist.

Lectionary Readings
Isaiah 11:1-10
Psalm 72:1-7, 18-19
Romans 15:4-13
Matthew 3:1-12

Call to Worship (adapted from Isaiah 11:1-10)

One: God's Anointed One is coming;
the spirit of wisdom is upon him.
All: There will be no rush to judgement,
And the powerless will know acceptance.
One: God's Anointed One is coming;
the spirit of understanding is upon him.
All: The poor will receive confidence
but the evil ones will be confronted.
One: God's Anointed One is coming;
the spirit of just action is upon him.
All: There will be peace at home,
and there will be peace abroad.
One: God's Anointed One is coming;
the spirit of faithfulness is upon him.
All: The earth will be full of the knowledge of God,
as the waters cover the sea.

Opening Prayer

One: Come with us on our Advent journey, O God;
All: give us the surprise of Mary, as we realize how much
you are ready to do for us.
One: Befriend us on our Advent journey, O God;

All: **give us the endurance of Joseph, as we realize how far you will journey with us.**

One: Stay with us on our Advent journey, O God;

All: **give us the wonderful joy of the angels, as we realize we can praise you in our own time.**

One: Keep us rooted on our Advent journey, O God;

All: **give us the practical response of the shepherds, even as the significance of Christ's birth fills us with awe.**

Or

Opening Prayer

One: We gather with the crowds on the bank of the Jordan River.

All: **Deep down, we know we lack God's Way for our lives.**

One: We listen with the crowds on the bank of the Jordan River.

All: **John is straightforward, down to earth, honest, and he calls on us to respond.**

One: We are moved to repent with the crowds on Jordan's bank.

All: **We know we cannot rely on what the world can give, to save us.**

One: We are aware of the presence of Jesus Christ on Jordan's bank.

All: **As John gives Jesus his due, so we, in our own time and situation, are ready to follow God's Promised One. Amen.**

Prayer of Affirmation (Confession)

One: This is the path we will follow, O God,

All: **the path of John the Baptist, prophet and visionary.**

One: When with the crowd, we are following the way of ease and self interest,

All: **give us the courage to speak out and act justly.**

One: When with the Pharisees and Sadducees, we are self centered and self righteous,

All: **help us to discover humility and compassion.**

One: When with the crowds, we are amazed that John would single out Jesus,

All: **give us the faith to acknowledge, and to follow, your Anointed One.**

Words of Assurance

One: Repentance is your call to us through the prophet John.

All: Answering the call to repentance requires our thorough reflection, a recognition of unfaithful practices, and resolute action...

Time of reflection...

One: In the decision to repent, pardon and peace are yours.

All: Thanks be to God! Amen.

Offering Prayer

One: Peace is your gift, O God:

All: the peace of generosity,
the peace of compassion,
the peace of recognition,
the peace of fellowship.

One: Bless these gifts, O God, which will convey the peace of Jesus Christ. Amen.

Or

Offering Prayer

One: John gave up an easy life and worldly security;

All: may we give gifts that mirror God's generosity.

One: John was moved to prophesy boldly and relevantly.

All: May our gifts be used to bring honesty and to combat procrastination.

One: John was not afraid to speak out against the powerful ones.

All: May our gifts threaten those who lean on tradition, and give a voice to those who are afraid to speak out for justice.

One: John was quick to give Jesus the central place.

All: May our gifts bring with them the inspiration and compassion of Jesus. Amen.

Commissioning

One: With us in our highest aspirations and most treasured dreams,
with us in our most tragic setbacks, with us in our deepest struggles:
journey with us now, God of the Advent season.

All: Deepen our faith,
show us the faithful way,
keep us faithfully on the way,
that we may respond to the One who is
the Way, the Truth, and the Life.

Or

Commissioning

One: Go from here as those who have heard the Baptist.

All: We will search for simplicity;
we will be ready to repent;
we will be prepared to receive God's Promised One;
we will know the joy of encountering Jesus Christ.

Advent 3

Lectionary Readings
Isaiah 35:1-10
Psalm 146: 5-10 or Luke 1:47-55
James 5:7-10
Matthew 11:2-11

Call to Worship (Isaiah 35, adapted)

One: When God's Anointed One comes,
All: the desert will rejoice, and flowers will bloom in the wasteland.
One: When God's Anointed One comes,
All: tired hands will receive new strength, and fearful ones will find fresh courage.
One: When God's Anointed One comes,
All: the lame will leap and dance, the blind will see.
One: When God's Anointed One comes,
All: the grieving and sorrowing will be forever free.

Opening Prayer

One: Your presence is revealed in the light of hope, O God. The light of hope shines brightly.
All: Joyfully we worship, for your graceful gift of Jesus is at hand.
One: The light of hope overcomes the darkness.
All: Joyfully we accept that the powerful ones and evil rulers will not have their own way.
One: The light of hope reveals the needs of home and community.
All: Joyfully we will work to support the downhearted and show friendship to those who are alone.
One: Your presence is revealed in the light of hope, O God.
All: The light of hope will shine out as we go on our Advent journey. Amen.

A Prayer for Life-Bringing (adapted from a prayer by John Baillie)

One: Through your Spirit, O God, you go to work with us, for us, and through us, whatever life may bring.
We experience setbacks.

All: O God, you enable us to use setbacks as a basis for opportunity.

One: We experience success.

All: O God, you enable us to use success as a stimulus to thanksgiving.

One: We experience loss.

All: O God, you enable us to use loss as a way to focus on hidden gifts.

One: We experience criticism.

All: O God, you enable us to use criticism as a part of positive self-examination.

One: We experience disappointment.

All: O God, you enable us to use disappointment as a means of finding patience.

One: We experience doubt.

All: O God, you enable us to experience doubt as a basis for forging faith.

Time of silent reflection…

Words of Assurance

One: You are with us, O God, in whatever life may bring, and you let us choose how we respond to the challenges of life.

All: As we respond with joy, with compassion, with humility, and with faith, we know you are with us, Loving God.

One: Pardon and peace are yours!

All: Thanks be to God! Amen.

Prayer of Confession

One: It takes a person like John the Baptist to call us to repentance.

All: It's hard to listen to those whose words come too close to home.

One: John came from a desert place and wore unusual clothes.

All: It's hard to pay attention to those who look or speak differently from ourselves.

One: John was direct; he called on the people of his day to turn their ways around, to repent.

All: It's hard to face up to your faults and failings, and tread a new path.

One: John was sure that the way to repentance lay in Jesus Christ,
Chosen One of God.

All: Jesus speaks hard words in the Gospel,
words that remind us of the cost of discipleship.

Time of silence...

Assurance of Forgiveness

One: We need the God-given assurance of John the Baptist to turn from indecision, indifference, and evil, to the life-giving ways that Jesus made clear.

All: O God, you are with us in this task.

One: Know the pardon and peace of God.

All: Amen.

Offering Prayer

One: For encouraging the sick,
for strengthening the fainthearted,
for touching the untouchable,
for bringing faith to the faithless,
for these reasons our gifts are given.

All: Bless them, O God. Bless them with the
Advent effectiveness of Jesus. Amen.

Commissioning

One: Go faithfully from this fellowship!

All: We go to search and not be defeated by doubt;
we go to serve, and not to be discouraged by a lack of response;
we go to create community, accepting that not all will feel at home;
we go to give thanks, yet not be overwhelmed at God's generosity.

One: We go to take the gift of Christ to heart,
and to respond with every fibre of our being.

Advent 4

Lectionary Readings
Isaiah 7: 10-16
Psalm 80:1-7, 17-19
Romans 1:1-7
Matthew 1:18-25

Call to Worship

One: God is with us!
All: We know God is with us; the prophets foretold God's Promised One.
One: God is with us!
All: We believe God is with us, for we have read the story of Joseph's acceptance of Mary, whom God had chosen.
One: God is with us!
All: We experience God with us, for our hearts are moved with the wonder of God's love, in the child who is to be born.
One: God is with us!
All: We will prove God is with us through words of compassion and deeds of caring.
One: God is with us.
All: Emmanuel, thanks be to God!

Opening Prayer

One: How amazing a beginning; a young woman is dramatically touched by God's Spirit.
All: We praise you, O God, for you assure us that life-changing words come at unexpected times.
One: How humble a beginning; a refugee family in makeshift accommodation.
All: We praise you, O God, for you remind us that your chosen ones are found in unforeseen situations.
One: How wonderful a beginning; the sky will be alive with angels singing.

All: **We praise you, O God, for you call us to open our hearts with wonder at the birth of your Promised One.**

One: How vulnerable a beginning; the powerful force of the state will stand opposed to the holy family.

All: **We praise you, O God, for you call us to work with the powerless and the persecuted.**
We praise you God, for the earth-changing event, which is the birth of Jesus Christ. Amen.

Prayer of Confession

One: You stand by us, O God, when our world is turned upside down.

All: **When our relationship with a loved one is tested in an unforeseen way, you are there!**

One: You stand by us, O God, when we are compelled to make changes.

All: **When we have to leave the known and trusted, when we venture out, you are there!**

One: You stand by us, O God, when our cherished dreams come to nothing.

All: **When we have to rethink our goals and priorities, you are there!**

One: You stand by us, O God, when the circumstances of life make us fearful.

All: **When we have lost foundations, tried and proved over the years, and search for secure ground, you are there!**

Words of Assurance

One: Accepting a new way for yourself is a series of small steps. It is not easy, but a beginning can be made.

All: **Living God, make holy our small and tentative beginnings, that we may come to love ourselves and others more.**

One: God is with you in your awesome task.

All: **Peace will be ours. Amen.**

Offering Prayer

One: When the world is ready for the coming of Jesus,
All: nations will talk peace, and back their words with actions.
One: When the church is ready for the coming of Jesus,
All: members will encourage each other, and share with the wider faith community.
One: When each one of us is ready for the coming of Jesus,
All: our struggle with security will be over, and we will know God's love for us and with us forever.
One: God will bless these gifts as we prepare for the coming of God's Promised One.
All: To God be glory and praise! Amen.

Commissioning

One: The challenge of God was experienced by Mary and Joseph.
All: It is there for us too!
One: The surprise of God was experienced by Mary and Joseph.
All: It is there for us too!
One: The peace of God was experienced by Mary and Joseph.
All: It is there for us too!
One: The love of God, in the baby Jesus,
was embraced by Mary and Joseph.
All: Emmanuel, God is with us too!

Christmas Eve/Day

Christmas, Proper 1 (Years A, B, C)

Lectionary Readings
Isaiah 9:2-7
Psalm 96
Titus 2:11-14
Luke 2:1-14 (15-20)

Call to Worship

One: The light shines in the darkness!
All: The praising angels around the shepherds at Bethlehem proclaim that light.
One: The light shines in the darkness!
All: The vulnerable babe, with his mother Mary, is the incarnation of the light.
One: The light shines in the darkness!
All: The powers of darkness, symbolized by Herod, cannot dim the light.
One: The light shines in the darkness!
All: The Way of Jesus Christ, just, courageous, forgiving, full of love, is an eternal beacon of light.

Opening Prayer

One: Come with the shepherds to Bethlehem.
All: Wonder, that so much love is set free in such a lowly child.
One: Come with the Magi to bring gifts to Mary and Joseph and Jesus.
All: Rejoice, that God's gift for all the ages, is given to you.
One: Understand with the family of Jesus, the powers that threaten and destroy.
All: Be glad that nothing can withstand the loving light of God.
One: Come with your family and friends to celebrate the birth of Jesus Christ.
All: Rejoice, that the spirit of God's Holy Child continues to reconcile, and to create new beginnings. Amen.

A Christmas Prayer of Confession

One: This is the wonder of Christmas worship, that we are together in fellowship and praise.

All: When we neglect to give you thanks and praise, O God, forgive us.

One: This is the joy of the Christmas season, that compassion flourishes and relationship is restored.

All: When we fail to reach out friendship's hand, O God, forgive us.

One: This is the inspiration of Christ's birth, that refugees and the poor are honoured.

All: When we see crying needs, and fail to meet them, O God, forgive us.

One: The glory of this holy time is clear. God's love is always there for us.

All: When we miss the significance of this love, open the door of the Bethlehem stable, and lead us to the light. Amen.

Assurance of Pardon

One: The coming of Jesus Christ is a turning point.

All; The light of his coming will be a turning point for each one of us, will enlighten our community of faith, and bring hope to our suffering world.

One: Know the peace of Christ.

All: Thanks be to God! Amen.

Offering Prayer

One: Enlighten with your love, O God, our homes, our families, and our friendships; may your love go to work through our gifts.

All: May the light of your Blessed One come at Christmas;
bring hope to the poor,
bring calm to the distressed,
bring peace to the troubled,
bring community to the lonely,
so that these cherished ones may receive
a blessing this Christmas, and in the days ahead. Amen.

Commissioning

One: The stable door is slightly open – look in:

All: see the gentle mother with her baby, know peace;
see the proud yet anxious father, feel the responsibility;
see the vulnerable and helpless babe, wonder at God's unceasing love.

Christmas Day/Eve

Proper 2 (A, B, C)

Lectionary Readings

Isaiah 62:6-12
Psalm 97
Titus 3:4-7
Luke 2:(1-7) 8-20

Call to Worship

One: Come, good friends, come to Bethlehem!

All: Come to Bethlehem and celebrate the newborn child with Mary and Joseph.

Females: Come and celebrate that God's symbol of love is a tiny, helpless baby.

Males: Come to Bethlehem and sing praises with the shepherds for what God has done.

One: Come to Bethlehem and fall silent in awe and wonder....(*silence*) Jesus is born, God's Word lives!

All: Praise to God. Alleluia, Alleluia!

Opening Prayer

One: We come to Bethlehem with Mary and Joseph;

All: we sense their worry and frustration, for they are far from home.

One: We are out in the fields with the shepherds;

All: we feel their awe and wonder as the sky echoes with singing.

One: We hurry to Bethlehem with the excited shepherds;

All: we know for ourselves that salvation has come in a tiny child.

One: We go back with these humble persons to their flocks;

All: we are aware that though everything seems the same, an earth-changing event has happened. And we rejoice! Amen.

Prayer of Confession

One: O God, that you would open our ears to hear the heavens alive with angels singing!

All: Then we might understand how you want us to praise you in the ordinary events of human life.

One: O God, that you would open our eyes to see your saving presence in a cradled, smiling, thumb sucking, little child!

All: Then we might understand that it is not the powerful who have all the answers, but the innocent and simple.

One: O God, that you would open our hearts to feel the vulnerability of a couple far away from their loved ones!

All: Then we might understand the deep needs of refugees, and those who have had to leave their homeland.

One: O God, that you would open our lips, to give voice to the praise and glory, which the shepherds gave to you!

All: Then we might understand that our Christmas celebrations are rooted in your gift of love, Jesus Christ.

Time of reflection…

Words of Assurance

One: We have found it so difficult to escape from the frenzied "commercial" Christmas, yet you, O Loving God, show us the calm and Holy way.

All: You will bring the peace of Christ to our stressed family circle;
you will bring the peace of Christ to our busy faith community;
you will bring the peace of Christ to those anxious in our neighbourhood;
you will bring the peace of Christ to our unsettled and terrorized world.

One: Each of you will know the peace of God's Holy Child, which passes all understanding.

All: Thanks be to God! Amen.

Offering Prayer

One: We offer our gifts, O God, remembering the gift of love we have received in Jesus Christ.

All: May these gifts bring a sense of wonder to those whose vision is limited;
may they bring peace to those who are in conflict;
may they bring friendship to those who are alone;
may they bring love to those who feel rejected.

One: Bless these our gifts, O God; bless the spirit of our giving; and bless those in whom these gifts will come alive.

All: Amen.

Commissioning

One: God's joy is yours!

All: We will enjoy our Christmas.

One: God's friendship is clear!

All: We will deepen our friendships.

One: God's peace is without limits!

All: We will let go our fear.

One: God's love is sure!

All: We will grow in love for one another.

Christmas Day

Proper 3 (A, B, C)

Lectionary Readings

Isaiah 52:7-10

Psalm 98

Hebrews 1:1-4, (5-12)

John 1:1-14

Call to Worship

One: O God, you give us hope beyond imagining,

All: hope, through the gift of Jesus, long hoped for by the prophets.

One: O God, you give us peace beyond imagining,

**All: peace, through the gift of Jesus,
whose way was to reconcile and bring calm.**

One: O God, you give us joy beyond happiness and celebration,

**All: joy, through the gift of Jesus, whose joy was known
by those released from fear and from despair.**

One: O God, you give us love beyond the deepest emotion,

**All: love, through the gift of Jesus, whose love for humankind
took him to a cross.**

Opening Prayer (adapted from John 1:1-14)

One: The Word was with God, the Word is with us now.

All: Thanks be to God for the birth of Jesus.

One: The light shines in the darkness, the darkness of our troubled world.

All: Thanks be to God for Jesus, the light-bringer.

One: Unrecognized, unappreciated, he went about his ministry.

All: Thanks be to God for Jesus, who brings change through love.

One: The children of God see his glory and rejoice.

**All: Thanks be to God for God's Word beyond words – graceful,
truthful, Jesus Christ. Amen.**

Prayer of Confession

One: Give us, Almighty God, the reassurance of the angel,
All: stilling the fear that is within us.
One: Give us, Living God, the peaceful chorus of the angels,
All: countering all that is at war within us, and within our relationships.
One: Give us, Compassionate God, the perception of the shepherds,
All: to search for the highest good in ourselves, and in others.
One: Give us, Loving God, the gentleness of Mary,
All: that it may reveal the harsh and impatient parts of ourselves.
Time of silent reflection...

Words of Assurance

One: You see clearly, in the light of Jesus Christ.
All: In the light of Christ, our darkness is exposed, confronted, rejected, and dispelled.
One: You are now forgiven people, people of the light!
God's peace is yours!
All: Thanks be to God! Amen.

Offering Prayer

One: We offer our gifts, remembering the gift of love
we have received in Jesus Christ.
All: Gifts to bring a sense of wonder, to those whose vision is limited;
gifts to bring peace to those who are in conflict;
gifts to bring love to those who feel unloved.
One: Bless these our gifts, O God, bless the spirit of our giving,
and bless those in whom these gifts will come alive. Amen.

Commissioning (from John 1)

One: Light shines in the darkness;
All: a light to all peoples.
One: This light is the light of truth;
All: the truth that enlightens us.
One: The Word became flesh,
All: and graciously lives with us.
Glory to God! Glory to God!

1st Sunday after Christmas

Lectionary Readings
Isaiah 63:7-9
Psalm 148
Hebrews 2:10-18
Matthew 2:13-23

Call to Worship

One: We welcome a new year.
All: O God, light up our way.
One: We face anxieties and fears.
All: O God, be light in our darkness.
One: We remember the troubled ones among family and friends.
All: O God, be the warm light of support.
One: In our world there is abuse, poverty, and fear.
All: O God, we will bring light to the dark places.
One: We will journey and venture as a faith community.
All: O God, your light will lead us forward.

A New Year Opening Prayer

One: The old year is nearly gone, and we give you thanks, O God. We thank you for courage in the tough times.
All: We thank you for joy in the good times.
One: We thank you for a challenge when the days were easy;
All: We thank you for endurance when the going was rough.
One: The new year comes close, and we have hope in our hearts. We hope for a strengthening of our faith community.
All: We hope for a deepening of our own faith.
One: We hope for a vision of truth and justice.
All: We hope for an end to poverty and powerlessness.
One: As you have blessed us in times past, O God, make us a blessing in the days that lie ahead.
All: Amen.

Prayer of Confession

One: The year is fast ending, O God, and we seek a new beginning.
Gracefully grant us the gift of careful reflection.
Where we have harboured bitterness,

All: give us the ability to put into words our deepest feelings.

One: Where we have nursed grudges,

All: give us the strength to let them go.

One: Where we have lacked the courage of our convictions,

All: give us the ability to stand up and be counted.

One: Where we have failed to work with others in community,

All: give us the sense of joy in a common cause.

One: Where we have questioned our life of faith,

All: give us the insight to turn doubts into fresh commitment.

One: Your grace is sufficient for us, O God.
And as we look to a new year, gracefully grant us a new vision.

**All: A vision of friendships deepened;
a vision of care, for ourselves and our relationships;
a vision of renewed service within the faith community;
a vision of a world where your realm is worked into reality.**

Time of silent reflection…

Assurance of Forgiveness

One: As we let go the past, O God, enable us to face the future
with confidence:

**All: ready to be open to new truths,
ready to accept fresh opportunities,
ready to seek new friendships,
ready to broaden our horizons,
ready to put aside old grudges,
ready to renew our faith in Jesus Christ.**

One: The peace of Christ is yours.

All: Thanks be to God! Amen.

Offering Prayer

One: Into your hands we present our gifts,
O God, for blessing;
All: **given for praise,**
given for support,
given for the powerless,
given justly,
given carefully,
given joyfully,
given in community,
given for global healing.
In Jesus' name we pray. Amen.

Commissioning

One: You are the sign towards the future, O God.
All: **You have no part in the superficial; neither have we.**
You have no time for the self-serving; neither have we.
You are on the side of the powerless; so are we.
You strengthen the faith community; so will we.
You are eternally hopeful; we will not look back.

Epiphany of the Lord

Lectionary Readings
Isaiah 60:1-6
Psalm 72:1-7, 10-14
Ephesians 3:1-12
Matthew 2:1-12

Call to Worship

One: A star shining brightly in the east;
All: discovered by those who have eyes to see
the unusual and the challenging.
One: A journey into unknown territory;
All: taken by those who have courage and curiosity.
One: An encounter with an evil person;
All: evil faced head on, yet resisted with care.
One: The Holy One recognized in spite of humble origins;
All: the glory and the gifts given to God's Chosen Child.
Let us worship God!

Opening Prayer

One: The light of God shines brightly;
All: it draws seekers to the source of all good.
One: The light of God shines brightly,
All: cutting through the darkness of sin and self serving.
One: The light of God shines brightly,
All: giving hope to all who live in the valley of the shadow.
One: The light of God shines brightly,
All: gloriously revealed in the life, death, and rising of Jesus Christ.

Prayer of Confession

One: When we have seen the challenging star, yet have
failed to set out on the journey,
All: God of Hope, forgive us!
One: When we have encountered the forces of evil, and
have compromised and gone along,

All: God of Conscience, forgive us!
One: When we have known worth and goodness, yet failed to
give the support of our best gifts,
All: God of Love, forgive us!
One: When we have realized the value of a community of friends,
yet have tried to go it alone,
All: God of the Church, forgive us!
Time of silent reflection…

Words of Assurance

One: As we reflect and confess, you address us, O God.
**All: In a resolve to trust you and change our ways, you encourage us;
as we set out again to live faithfully, you journey with us.**
One: Pardon and peace are yours.
All: Thanks be to God! Amen.

Offering Prayer

One: The gifts of gold and frankincense and myrrh
were signs of commitment to God's gift of love.
**All: These gifts are signs of commitment to the faith community.
Bless them as your Word is heard and your people are inspired.
Bless them as the lonely find companionship,
and the powerless find partners.
Bless them as the oppressed find justice,
and the bereaved know renewed hope.
Bless them as a token of all we can give and be in Jesus Christ.**

Commissioning

One: We leave this church prepared to act with Christ.
**All: Alert for those whose situations are difficult, whose outlook is bleak;
ready to stand beside the outcast;
prepared to stay the course beside the suffering ones
with resources of empathy, patience, and abundant hope.**
One: Go with us, loving and compassionate God.
Enable us to be your listening ear, and your well-tuned instrument
for justice and for care.

1st Sunday after the Epiphany

Baptism of the Lord

Lectionary Readings
Isaiah 42:1-9
Psalm 29
Acts 10:34-43
Matthew 3:13-17

Call to Worship

One: Let us journey to the Jordan River,
All: crossing place of the people of Israel when they came into the promised land.
One: Let us journey to the Jordan River,
All: and stand with the crowds who confess their sins, and are baptized by John.
One: Let us journey to the Jordan River,
All: and watch with awe as Jesus comes to be baptized.
One: Let us journey to the Jordan River,
All: and realize our responsibility as members of the "Community of the Baptized."

Opening Prayer

One: Give us the single-mindedness of John the Baptist.
All: John is ready to speak out for God's just and sharing realm.
One: Give us the straightforwardness of John the Baptist.
All: John is not afraid to identify and condemn the evil ones.
One: Give us the insight of John the Baptist.
All: John recognizes Jesus, and testifies to his spiritual significance.
One: Give us the humility of John the Baptist.
All: John sees the greatness of Jesus, and responds by serving him.
One: Give us the determination of John the Baptist, in our Christian discipleship.
All: We will risk and venture unafraid. Amen.

Prayer of Confession

One: We thank you, God, for your call to be "the People of God,"
All: but we confess, we have not listened faithfully, nor acted boldly.
One: We thank you for your call to follow Jesus,
All: but we confess, we have been slow to see Jesus in our friends and family, let alone in a stranger.
One: We thank you for the call to be "The Church,"
All: but we have put limits of what "Church" means, and denied its potential.
One: We thank you for the global impact of Christ's ministry,
All: but we have found it difficult to look beyond our local needs and concerns.

Words of Assurance

One: "Repent!" was the call of John the Baptist.
Are you ready to make a fresh start?
All: We are ready to turn our lives around:
to forgive freely,
to give generously,
to support compassionately,
to work in faith community,
to act justly,
to think globally,
to risk and to venture out.
One: You are ready to bring change in the Way of Jesus Christ.
Pardon and peace are yours!
All: Thanks be to God! Amen.

Offering Prayer

One: What can we offer to the One who offered himself for baptism by John at the Jordan?

All: We can offer our best gifts: our time, our talent, and our treasure, for Jesus gave his best to the world.

One: And will our gifts be used faithfully and wisely?

All: They will be well used, if the life pattern of Jesus is followed, and the powers of darkness challenged.

One: God will bless all our gifts, as they are put to work in the spirit of Jesus.

All: Thanks be to God! Amen.

Commissioning

One: Remember the common ties that hold you in baptism!

All: We recall our common participation in the community of faith.

One: Remember the needs that are brought home to you.

All: We are challenged to use our common talents to meet those needs.

One: Remember the wisdom of the saints who have gone before you.

All: We will draw on their wisdom, and take courage from their endurance.

One: Remember the Holy Spirit stands with you.

All: In the power of the Spirit, there are no obstacles that cannot be overcome!

2nd Sunday after the Epiphany

Lectionary Readings
Isaiah 49:1-7
Psalm 40:1-11
1 Corinthians 1:1-9
John 1:29-42

Call to Worship

One: You can trust God.
All: In the shifting sands of life, God is the rock.
One: You can trust God.
All: Among the conflicting values and views, God's Word clarifies.
One: You can trust God.
All: Faced with self-serving opportunities, God turns us towards the needy.
One: You can trust God.
All: When the world confuses and threatens, God's Spirit restores peace.

Opening Prayer

One: Loving God, you are light in our darkness.
All: When we doubt our ability to affect change in the world, show us the way.
One: Help us to experience the joy of others.
All: In the celebration of life, may our laughter be heard, O God.
One: Help us to sense the loneliness of others.
All: In the hard places of life, may our friendship be felt, O God.
One: Help us to feel the hurt of others.
All: In the testing situations of life, may we stand with the troubled ones, O God.
One: Help us to bring hope to others.
All: When the outlook is bleak, may we witness to the Risen Christ, O God. Amen.

Prayer of Confession

One: Loving God, you are light in our darkness.

All: When we struggle to find the truth, or tell the truth, enlighten us.

One: Loving God, you are light in our darkness.

All: When we struggle to find words of support or comfort, encourage us.

One: Loving God, you are light in our darkness.

All: When we shy away from the just cause or from merciful action, challenge us.

One: Loving God, you are light in our darkness.

All: When we hang back from faith community needs, prompt us to participation.

Time of silence…

Words of Assurance

One: The light of Jesus Christ puts our personal and church life in perspective.

All: We will accept the freedom, the tough choices, and the determination that the inspiration of Jesus grants us.

One: A new way has opened up; pardon and peace are ours.

All: Thanks be to God! Amen.

Offering Prayer

One: Through your gifts, change will take place.

All: Through our gifts, friendship will be experienced;
through our gifts, joy will come to life;
through our gifts, healing will be possible;
through our gifts, community will be created;
through our gifts, freedom will be experienced.

One: Bless these our gifts, O God. Amen.

Commissioning

One: Trust God's Anointed One to go with you.

All: O Lamb of God, hold us securely in the most testing moments.
O Lamb of God, enable us to carefully support those who are suffering.
O Lamb of God, empower us as a faith community to stand beside those who are alone.
O Lamb of God, grant us your peace – your strengthening, active peace.

3rd Sunday after the Epiphany

Lectionary Readings
Isaiah 9:1-4
Psalm 27:1, 4-9
1 Corinthians 1:10-18
Matthew 4:12-23

Call to Worship

One: Jesus will not be defeated.
All: In our moments of despair, he creates hope.
One: Jesus gives us confidence for friendship.
All: When we are alone, he encourages us towards community.
One: Jesus is the strong foundation.
All: When our faith seems unfounded, he enables us to trust.
One: Jesus is our light in the darkness.
All: When the journey fills us with fear, he walks with us.

Opening Prayer

One: This is the moment of praise:
All: praise to the God who has created us, and
sustains us, in joy and in sorrow.
One: This is the moment of trust:
All: trust in the God who remains faithful, as
the strong ones change, as the years change.
One: This is the moment of community:
All: community of those who profess their faith
in Jesus Christ, in word and in compassionate
work together.
One: This is the moment of hope:
All: hope for those in the midst of life's storms,
hope for those who feel the grip of despair,
hope for those who fear the untried and the unknown.
This is the moment of God with God's people.
Glory to God. Amen.

Prayer of Thanksgiving and Confession

One: We thank you, O God, for the opportunity to follow Jesus, your Chosen One.

All: We confess our discipleship has lacked understanding, faithfulness, and enthusiasm.

One: We thank you, O God, for the opportunity to bring closer to the kingdom of justice, love, and peace that Jesus proclaimed.

All: We confess that our own concerns have taken priority; we have been slow to advance the freedom-bringing way.

One: We thank you, O God, for the opportunity to learn, work, and worship with fellow members of this faith community.

All: We confess that we have been slow to use the influence of our faith community to change our neighbourhood for good.

One: We thank you, O God, for the resources and talents that are ours.

All: We confess that we have been reluctant to share our gifts with those poor in resources and opportunity.

Week of Prayer for Christian unity

One: We thank you, O God, for the chance to work with other faith communities to proclaim the Good News of Jesus Christ.

All: We confess that we have been suspicious of other faith groups, and have hung back from accepting them as full partners.

Time of silence…

Words of Assurance

One: The time for change has arrived!

**All: Take from us, O God, the reluctance to get involved,
the unwillingness to cooperate with others,
and the arrogance that insists that we
have the whole truth.**

One: In an openness to new truth, in an enthusiasm to work with others, in a willingness to go the extra mile in faith, new horizons open up, fresh starts are possible. Accept the peace of God!

All: Thanks be to God. Amen.

Offering Prayer

One: Touch us with your Spirit, O God;

All: touch us as we give, that our giving may reflect faithful discipleship.

One: Touch us as our gifts go to work, O God;

All: touch us in the way of Christ,
that the struggling ones may find freedom.

One: Touch us with the will to bring change,

All: that the despairing ones may find hope,
and the lonely find community.

One: Come Holy Spirit, bless our gifts. Amen

Commissioning

One: Call us to discipleship, O God.

All: As disciples we will follow Jesus, the hope of our calling.

One: Call us to discipleship, O God.

All: As disciples we will take the Way of Jesus seriously.

One: Call us to discipleship, O God.

All: As disciples we will speak of our faith with sensitivity.

One: Call us to discipleship, O God.

All: As disciples we will search out the needs that surround us.

One: Call us to discipleship, O God.

All: As disciples we will promote the just and generous sharing of basic human needs.

4th Sunday after the Epiphany

Lectionary Readings
Micah 6:1-8
Psalm 15
1 Corinthians 1:18-31
Matthew 5:1-12

Call to Worship

One: This is the place of worship and of praise.
All: We are glad to be here!
One: These are the friends who are with us in joy and in sorrow.
All: We rejoice in their presence!
One: This is the faith community through which compassion and justice become possible.
All: We will accept the responsibility.
One: This is the Good News that Jesus proclaimed in deed and word.
All: O Most Gracious and Loving God, we will follow your Way.

Opening Prayer

One: What does God require of us?
All: That we give thanks for creation, for family, for opportunity, and for worship.
One: What does God require of us?
All: That we remember God's presence, and rejoice that God has a word for us.
One: What does God require of us?
All: That we encourage each other in the Spirit of Jesus Christ.
One: What does God require of us?
All: That we do justice, love kindness, and walk humbly with our God. Amen.

A Reflective, Call-to-Action Prayer (Confession)

One: Jesus blessed children, those who had no possessions, no money, and no control over their own destiny.

All: You call us to care for children, for the disadvantaged, for all who rely on others for the good life.

One: Jesus blessed the outcasts in his society: the lepers, and the mentally challenged.

All: You call us to bring today's outcasts into our community, and to share our resources with them.

One: Jesus blessed the family of Lazarus, and the widow who gave her last coin.

All: You call us to comfort those who have lost loved ones, and support those who have lost their independence.

One: Jesus blessed his friends, the disciples, even when they let him down.

All: You call us to be open to God's blessing, especially when God seems absent, and we feel at a loss.

Time of silent reflection…

Words of Assurance

One: You bless us, O God, as we realize your good feelings for us, and ask to be a blessing – among the most vulnerable, with the despairing, and with those who are afraid.

All: In counting our blessings, in giving our blessing, we know pardon and peace.

One: You will be blessed!

All: Thanks be to God. Amen.

Offering Prayer

One: O God, Great and Eternal Giver, we rejoice in your generosity to us from our first day, to this day.
Enable us to share your generosity with the poor:

All: those without adequate food or shelter,
those in poor health,
those poor in friendship and family,
those poor in their life of faith.

One: We offer these gifts for blessing, in the name of Jesus, who blessed the poor and said, "theirs is the Kingdom of Heaven." Amen.

Commissioning

One: You will be a blessing!

All: We will encourage those poor in spirit;
we will comfort those who mourn;
we will honour the humble;
we will recognize the faithful;
we will strive to be merciful;
we will learn from those pure in heart;
we will follow the path of peace;
we will count ourselves among those
who follow the demanding Way of Jesus Christ.

One: You *will* be a blessing!

5th Sunday after the Epiphany

Lectionary Readings
Isaiah 58:1-9a, (9b-12)
Psalm 112:1-9, (10)
1 Corinthians 2:1-12, (13-16)
Matthew 5:13-20

Call to Worship

One: People of God, rejoice in God's presence!
All: As we praise and pray, God is with us.
One: People of God, rejoice in this faith community!
All: As we support each other, as we reach out a helping hand, God is with us.
One: People of God, rejoice in your Christian faith!
All: As we follow the way of Jesus, as we proclaim his Good News, God is with us.

Opening Prayer

One: You are keepers of God's promise.
All: We rejoice in this opportunity to worship.
One: You are keepers of God's promise.
All: We support each other through prayer and action.
One: You are keepers of God's promise.
All: We look out for the needs of our local community.
One: You are keepers of God's promise.
All: We have known God's promise, wonderfully kept, in the life, death, and rising of Jesus. Amen.

A Prayer for Zest in our Lives (Confession)

One: Give us, O God, your zest for life. When the routine of everyday life dominates and oppresses us,
All: give us, O God, your zest for life; free us up to follow in fresh and exciting directions.
One: When the worries of our situation seem never ending,

All: **give us, O God, your zest for life, the will to seek help, the courage to make difficult choices.**

One: When the troubles of a friend or family member weigh on us,

All: **give us, O God, your zest for life, that we may encourage and inspire.**

One: When the way of the church seems uninspiring and dull,

All: **give us, O God, your zest for life, the vision of a joyful fellowship, the chance to share in new faith enterprises.**

Time of silence...

Words of Assurance

One: Like salt, like yeast, your influence is silent,
yet strong within us, O God.

All: **As we feel our confidence restored,**
as we sense our hope renewed,
as we realize the power for good that is ours
in Christian fellowship, an active peace is ours.

One: Pardon and peace is God's will for you.

All: **Thanks be to God. Amen.**

Offering Prayer

One: Through your Holy Spirit, O God, you gently yet
effectively go to work.

All: **Into the life of this community, you breathe friendship;**
into the work of this community, you breathe energy;
into the suffering ones of this community, you breathe compassion;
into the challenges of this community, you breathe hope.
And into those supported by the gifts of this community,
the needy of this city, the powerless of our world,
you breathe encouragement.

One: We will be partners with the Spirit, we will work to bring change.
Amen.

Commissioning

One: God brings you true happiness.

**All: Happiness comes as God's Word is heeded,
as God's commandments are followed.
Happiness arises as God's people are courageous,
as the powerful ones are confronted.
Happiness is rooted in the hearts of the faithful,
in a response that banishes fear.
Happiness is spread with the recognition of need,
with the response of generosity.
Happiness finds a focus in Jesus Christ,
but is there for all humanity.**

6th Sunday after the Epiphany

Proper 1

If this is the Sunday before Ash Wednesday, this Proper may be replaced, in those churches using Transfiguration readings on this day, by the readings for the Last Sunday after the Epiphany.

Lectionary Readings
Deuteronomy 30:15-20
Psalm 119:1-8
1 Corinthians 3:1-9
Matthew 5:21-37

Call to Worship

One: Come from homes and work to praise God.
All: We are ready!
One: Come from the rough places of life to worship God.
All: We will find friendship!
One: Come remembering all we have received, to give thanks to God.
All: Our joy is great!
One: Come into the fellowship of this church, to find a common purpose.
All: In Christ's community we are strong!

Opening Prayer

One: You surprise us as we come to worship, O God.
All: The smile of a fellow worshipper, the feeling evoked by a favorite hymn, remind us that we belong.
One: You delight us as we come to worship, O God.
All: The laughter of boys and girls, the greeting of old friends, lifts our spirits.
One: You challenge us as we come to worship, O God.
All: The needs of the faith community, the needs of despairing ones far from here, call us to action.
One: Your love enfolds us as we come to worship, O God.
All: Your love, compassionately clear in Jesus; your love lifted up on a cross, endures and will endure. Amen.

A Prayer for Reconciliation (Confession)

One: Bring us together, Loving God; show us the path to reconciliation.

All: Where hasty words have hurt, bring us together in peace, to give and accept apology.

One: Bring us together, Loving God, show us the path to reconciliation.

All: Where the sting of rejection has caused hard feelings, bring us together with friendship to make a fresh start.

One: Bring us together Loving God, show us the path to reconciliation.

All: Where life has been smooth sailing for one and hell for another, bring us together to listen to the stories, and to support those sorely tested.

One: Bring us together, Loving God, show us the path to reconciliation.

All: Where division has split the Christian community, bring us together with faith, to pray and to work together.

Words of Assurance

One: God will give the motivation for change,
the will to be reconciled. God will hear your heartfelt prayers.

All: We will speak of our deepest conflicts, we will give voice to hidden grudges, name the objects of our hate.

One: God will hear you out, and make clear a way to understanding and new beginnings.

All: We recognize that change will not be easy, that old hatreds die hard, but change we will!

One: The way to peace will open up for you, God's pardon will be yours.

All: Thanks be to God! Amen.

Offering Prayer

One: Bless these gifts, O God;

All: through them the ordinary becomes sacred,
through them the trials of life may be borne,
through them the joys of life may be celebrated,
through them the fearful may be filled with hope,
through them the Good News may be proclaimed,
and the Way of Jesus honoured. Amen.

Commissioning

One: You have life choices before you, as you leave this church.

All: We will choose the life that is joyful and fulfilling;
we will choose the life that goes beyond the well-known borders;
we will choose the life that seeks the way of reconciliation;
we will choose the life that contributes to community;
we will choose the life that shares with generosity;
we will choose the life that is lived as a disciple of Jesus Christ.

7th Sunday after the Epiphany

Proper 2

If this is the Sunday before Ash Wednesday, this Proper may be replaced, in those churches using Transfiguration readings on this day, by the readings for the Last Sunday after the Epiphany.

Lectionary Readings
Leviticus 19:1-2, 9-18
Psalm 119:33-40
1 Corinthians 3:10-11, 16-23
Matthew 5:38-48

Call to Worship

One: The diffuse light of the sunrise, a sign;
All: Christ's hopeful light, ending the darkness.
One: The lightbeam from a lighthouse, a sign;
All: Christ's light of security in a fast changing world.
One: The clear beam from a flashlight, a sign;
All: Christ's revealing light, exposing the ways of selfishness and greed.
One: The gentle light of a candle, a sign;
All: Christ, the Light of the World for his time, for our time, and all time beyond.

Opening Prayer

One: What a generous nature you have, O God!
All: You have given us gifts in creation without number, you have covered us with your starry sky.
One: What a generous nature you have, O God!
All: You have set us in families, and given us the joy of parents, grandparents, and children.
One: What a generous nature you have, O God!
All You have shown us the power of forgiveness, the sense of not repaying wrong with wrong.
One: What a generous nature you have, O God!
All: You have graced us, your Church, with opportunities for working together.

One: What a generous nature you have, O God!

All: You have given us Jesus your Anointed One,
whose life values, and death on the cross,
resound with your generosity. Amen.

Prayer of Confession

One: It seems impossible to love our enemies, O God;
they have hurt and humiliated us.

All: You show us that revenge does not work out.

One: It seems impossible to love our enemies, O God;
they have taken advantage and laugh at us.

All: You show us that we have to see their point of view.

One: It seems impossible to love our enemies, O God;
they undermine our self confidence.

All: You show us that peace can be shared between us.

One: It seems impossible to love our enemies, O God;
they expose our failings and shortcomings.

All: In Jesus, you have shown us that with love
nothing is impossible.

Time for silent reflection…

Words of Assurance

One: Jesus says, "Love your enemies and pray
for those who persecute you."

All: We will take these words to heart, and remember
when anger and thoughts of revenge rule.

One: Jesus says, "turn the other cheek."

All: It is so hard to do this, O God, but we believe it will work.

One: Pardon and peace are yours.

All: Thanks be to God! Amen.

Offering Prayer

One: Our gifts are blessed through your Spirit, O God.

All: They find sadness and bring comfort;
they find despair and bring hope;
they find persons in a rut and bring freedom;

they find talent and expose it for all to see;
they find narrow-mindedness and bring fresh insights,
the same way Jesus did! Amen.

Commissioning

One: You, O God, show us the pattern of a lifestyle
that is in tune with your love for all humankind:
All: a lifestyle overflowing with your forgiveness,
a lifestyle marked with compassion,
a lifestyle characterized by sharing,
a lifestyle nurtured in family,
a lifestyle maturing in community,
a lifestyle concerned with wholeness and healing,
a lifestyle global in its generosity.
One: A lifestyle following the pattern of Jesus.

8th Sunday after the Epiphany

Proper 3

If this is the Sunday before Ash Wednesday, this Proper can be replaced,, in those churches using Transfiguration readings on this day, by the readings for the Last Sunday after the Epiphany.

Lectionary Readings

Isaiah 49:8-16a
Psalm 131
1 Corinthians 4:1-5
Matthew 6:24-34

Call to Worship

One: Come before God in prayer;
All: our prayers will be full of thanksgiving for God's graciousness to us.
One: Rejoice in God's Word for us today;
All: save us from merely listening, show us how we can put the Word to work.
One: Take your lead from the saints;
All: we have such a fine example in God's "down to earth" holy ones.

Opening Prayer

One: Have done with worry and anxiety!
All: God, who cares for the birds and the wildflowers, cares for you.
One: Have done with worry and anxiety!
All: Speak freely of the concerns that weigh heaviest on your heart.
One: Have done with worry and anxiety!
All: Take action to face those persons and problems that impact on you.
One: Have done with worry and anxiety!
All: Bring your worries and anxieties to God in prayer. God will not leave you in the lurch. Thanks be to God! Amen.

A Prayer for Good Stewardship (Confession)

One: You call us to be good stewards, O God, you call us to prayer.

All: Where our prayer has been selfish or without imagination, forgive us!

One: You call us to be good stewards, O God, you call us to worship.

All: Where our worship has lacked joy or enthusiasm, forgive us!

One: You call us to be good stewards, O God, you call us to learning.

All: Where our learning has lacked questioning or a community, forgive us!

One: You call us to be good stewards, O God, you call us to share our treasure.

All: Where our sharing has lacked concern for the wider church or a spirit of generosity, forgive us!

One: You call us to be good stewards, O God, you call us to share our skills and gifts.

All: Where our sharing has lacked a willingness to own our talent, or to risk sharing it, forgive us!

One: You call us to be good stewards, O God, you call us to follow Jesus.

All: Where our discipleship has been halfhearted or lacked adventure, forgive us!

Time of silence...

Assurance of Pardon

One: We recall the words of Jesus,

All: "Well done, you good and faithful servant, enter into the joy of your Lord."

One: The words of Jesus are for all good stewards.

All: We will take them to heart. Thanks be to God. Amen.

Offering Prayer

One: What can we offer to God who has made us all we are,
and given us all we have?

**All: We will offer the response of worship and thanksgiving;
we will offer minds ready for new truth;
we will offer hearts ready for compassionate service;
we will offer a readiness to work for those denied justice or
a fair opportunity;**

and we will offer these gifts of money, so that others can serve in the way of Jesus Christ.

One: And God will accept your gifts and bless them.

All: To God be the glory! Amen.

Commissioning

One: Serve God joyfully, carefully, and without holding back!

All: God will open us up to new experiences,
and take the limitations of the past away.

One: Serve God unselfishly; there are many in your neighbourhood,
and overseas, crying out for a fair chance.

All: God will give us the confidence to achieve so much.

One: Serve God wholeheartedly, for he gave us Jesus, his Precious One!

All: God will strengthen our faith, and our determination to follow as contemporary disciples.

One: You have been called!

All: We are ready to serve!

9th Sunday after the Epiphany

Lectionary Readings
Deuteronomy 11:18-21, 26-28
Psalm 31:1-5, 19-24
Romans 1:16-17, 3:22b-28, (29-31)
Matthew 7:21-29

Call to Worship

One: The worship of God is a blessing.
All: We rejoice that we can praise and pray.
One: The word of God is a blessing.
All: We listen and we stand ready to obey.
One: The way of God is a blessing.
All: We are glad to help others along that way.
One: The people of God are a blessing.
All: We give thanks that we can support and share in this faith community.

Opening Prayer

One: The Good News is news to be trusted.
**All: In the clutter of everyday views and opinions,
we will find the faithful path.**
One: The Good News is news that brings freedom.
**All: The powers of darkness and discouragement
will not win through.**
One: The Good News is news of salvation.
**All: Nothing worthwhile, and no one who follows Christ's lead
will be lost or forgotten.**
One: The Good News is news about Jesus Christ.
**All: God's love shines through him, in all human experience and time.
Amen.**

A Prayer for a Strong Foundation (Confession)

One: Give us the strong foundation, O God:
All: your peace, which holds us strong in the storms of life.
One: Give us the strong foundation, O God:
All: your confidence, which endures when our cherished beliefs are shaken.
One: Give us the strong foundation, O God:
All: your compassion, which reaches out to the lonely and unloved.
One: Give us the strong foundation, O God:
All: your love, that time and the events in time cannot defeat.

Time of reflection…

Words of Assurance

One: You know our uncertainty and wavering, O God;
All: you give us confidence to face the necessary decisions.
One: You know our shortsightedness and timidity;
All: you give us perspective and courage.
One: And so in the storms we experience, in the faith community, within our families and ourselves we will not fear.
All: You, O God, are our strength and guide.
You will never let us down. Thank you! Amen.

Offering Prayer

One: The deeds of Christ are reflected
in those who are touched by these gifts.
All: The heartfelt storms are stilled,
the powerless are given confidence,
the sick are visited,
the lonely are supported,
the hungry are fed,
the evil ones are confronted,
and God's word is heard.
One: These are powerful gifts.
All: Thanks be to God! Amen.

Commissioning

One: In the storms of life,
All: you are rock solid, O God.
One: When we are unsure,
All: you put us straight, O God.
One: When our faith falters,
All: you place the cross of Jesus before us, O God.
One: When time threatens us,
All: your eternal love surrounds us, O God.
We will not fear!

Last Sunday after the Epiphany

Transfiguration Sunday

Lectionary Readings

Exodus 24: 12-18
Psalm 2 or Psalm 99
2 Peter 1:16-21
Matthew 17:1-9

Call to Worship

One: The Glory of God is around us;
All: God is with us in the most testing times.
One: The Glorious God reveals truth to us;
All: in Jesus, we have the words that count, and the example to follow.
One: The Glorious God is to be praised;
All: we will joyfully bring our prayers, our hymns, and our thanksgivings to God.
Let us worship God!

Opening Prayer

One: It is a mystery, O God, your creation of this wonderful world.
All: We come before you, thankful for the gift of life.
One: It is a mystery, O God, your presence known by the people of ancient days.
All: We come before you as a chosen people.
One: It is a mystery, O God, your gradually revealed love for all humankind.
All: We come before you, rejoicing that your love endures.
One: It is a mystery, O God, your supreme gift to the world in Jesus Christ.
All: We come before you as those whose saving acts will reflect the Saviour. Amen.

Prayer of Confession

One: This is an awesome place; we stand on Holy Ground.

All: Forgive us, O God, when we take our worship and service for granted.

One: This is an awesome place; we are inspired by a Holy Book.

All: Forgive us, O God, when we ignore your word for us and our faith community.

One: This is an awesome place, and we are called to sacred tasks.

All: Forgive us, O God, when our response is casual and partial.

One: This is an awesome place, and we follow an awesome Christ.

All: Forgive us, O God, when we resist Christ's call to compassion, to acceptance, and to justice.

Time of silence…

Words of Assurance

One: Let us receive the inspiration of God.

**All: In your Spirit, O God, the ordinary is transformed into the Holy;
in your Spirit, O God, all that is unworthy is left in the past;
in your Spirit, O God, the future will be faced without fear.**

One: In God's Spirit, peace and a new way will be yours.

All: Thanks be to God. Amen.

Offering Prayer

One: Beyond our understanding or imagining,
you are for us and with us, O God.

All: These gifts are a pledge of our loyalty to you.

One: Grant us wisdom and common sense as we use
all you have entrusted to us;

**All: that your name may be glorified,
and the Way of Jesus carefully followed. Amen.**

Commissioning

One: Rejoice that your God is Holy and inspiring!

All: We have worshipped the Creator and Sustainer of all that lives and moves.

One: Bring glory to the champion of the powerless, the Eternally Merciful One!

All: God has worked through the life of Jesus, and the compassion of some unspectacular saints.

One: Go from this church to serve God in your own time and situation!

All: We will serve faithfully in our own place, and with our church friends.
We will serve the suffering whose need is plain, but whose names we will never know.

Lent 1

Lectionary Readings
Genesis 2:15-17, 3:1-7
Psalm 32
Romans 5:12-19
Matthew 4:1-11

Call to Worship

One: We gather with the disciples.
The enthusiastic crowds of Judea and Galilee are behind us.
All: God fills us with thankfulness for Jesus: skilled healer, wise teacher, close friend.
One: The highway to Jerusalem stretches ahead of us.
All: God gives us courage to walk the challenging Lenten Way with Jesus, the Chosen One.
One: At the end of the journey there is a hill and a cross.
All: God calls on us to wonder at what sacrificial love will do, and to respond to Christ's love in practical ways.

Opening Prayer

One: God loves this congregation so much, and has gifted us Jesus;
All: through Jesus we are encouraged to bring our heartfelt praise and prayer to God.
One: God loves the wider church so much, and has gifted us Jesus;
All: through Jesus we are challenged to broaden our vision of cooperation and responsibility.
One: God loves the world so much, and has gifted us Jesus;
All: through Jesus we are prepared to serve those most at risk, both near and far away.
One: God loves each one of us so much, and has gifted us Jesus;
All: through Jesus, we have the promise of salvation and of eternal life. Thanks be to God! Amen.

Prayer of Confession for Lent

One: Let us go out with Jesus to the desert, and know his temptations; the Devil said, "Turn these stones into bread."

All: Food and drink will only go so far to satisfy; we need God's Word, the spiritual food.

One: The Devil said, "Throw yourself down from this pinnacle of the Temple."

All: We do not need miracles to save us; we will find God as we loyally serve day by day.

One: The Devil said, "All the world's power and influence you need, I will give to you."

All: We do not need power over others; rather we seek to work with others for justice, freedom, and peace.

Time of silence…

Assurance of Pardon

One: The darkness will be overcome by the Light.

**All: As we open our eyes to the subtle power of evil,
as we confront the evil powers and name them,
as we find strength to recognize the evil in ourselves and overcome it, peace will be ours.**

One: Rejoice! Evil is powerless; peace is your reality.

All: Thanks be to God! Amen.

Offering Prayer

One: These gifts will be blessed by you, O Loving God.

**All: Blessed through honest questioning,
blessed through a quest for meaning,
blessed through gentle encouragement,
blessed through serving the downhearted,
blessed through facing temptation,
blessed in common endeavour.**

One: Confidently we offer these gifts, O God, for you have blessed us in Jesus. Amen.

Commissioning

One: Begin your Lenten journey:

All: We will listen for God's call;
we will respond with the commitment Jesus made clear;
we will endure the hard places and the struggle;
we will rejoice in the victory that lies beyond the cross.

Lent 2

Lectionary Readings

Genesis 12:1-4a
Psalm 121
Romans 4:1-5, 13-17
John 3:1-17 or Matthew 17:1-9

Call to Worship

One: We gather as a people for whom faith matters.
All: O God, deepen our faith.
One: We gather as a people rejoicing in memory.
All: O God, hallow our tradition.
One: We gather as a people committed to the church.
All: O God, give us joy in serving Jesus Christ.
One: We gather as a people who proclaim the Good News.
All: In word and deed, your justice and compassion shine out, O God.

Opening Prayer

One: Give us a spiritual rebirth, O God.
All: As we read the Word and receive inspiration, there is joy.
One: Give us a spiritual rebirth, O God.
All: As we encounter the saints and follow their example, we take courage.
One: Give us a spiritual rebirth, O God.
All: As we feel support in community and give of our talents, our faith comes alive.
One: Give us a spiritual rebirth, O God.
All: As we as we reflect on Jesus Christ, and renew our commitment, we know peace. Amen.

An Encounter with Jesus – A Confessional Visualization

Today's Gospel reading tells of the encounter of Nicodemus, a Jewish community leader, with Jesus. Nicodemus is a searcher after the truth and he meets God's Chosen One – a wise counsellor, a perceptive listener – a spiritual person. The result is a challenge to be reborn.

I want you to relax now... close your eyes... get comfortable... banish the clutter of thoughts about work and home, from your mind, and imagine you are walking down a dusty, unpaved street in a small middle Eastern town of 2,000 years ago. It's the evening, it's dark and it's quiet... in the distance a dog barks and you hear a child cry out.

In front of you is a small, square, whitewashed house. Your heartbeat quickens as you approach and then knock on a well-worn door. "Come in," says a voice from inside. With some hesitation you enter. In front of you, sitting cross-legged on a low patterned mat is Jesus. He looks just as you always imagined he would look.

Jesus beckons you to sit down, and as he does his eyes meet yours, and you experience an extraordinary sense of being known, accepted, appreciated, and loved in a way that goes beyond anything you have experienced in your life so far.

"What is on your heart that you long to tell me?" Jesus asks.

Time of reflection...

As you reflect in Jesus' presence, you are able to put words around some of your deepest feelings and thoughts.

He speaks again, gently. "You are a gifted child of God. What untapped gifts, what talents kept hidden, what submerged skills are you called on to use, to bring freedom and joy to others?"

Time of reflection...

The eyes of Jesus never leave yours. "What one thing can you do in company with your faithful friends to bring closer God's realm of compassion, justice, inclusion, and peace?"

Time of reflection...

You know your time with Jesus is at an end.

Quietly, you prepare yourself to leave, but Jesus motions you to stay. Again his eyes meet yours – not a word is spoken, but you sense joy flooding in on you – burdens are lifted, challenges are clarified; the way ahead will not be easy but you are ready to set out. Jesus blesses you.

"My peace I leave with you – still your fears."
You leave his presence. You are at peace. Amen.

Offering Prayer

One: New life is your gift to us, O God; may these gifts bring new life.
All: Hope to the despairing,
confidence to the faltering,
peace to the suffering,
faith to the doubting,
a word to the questioning,
a light for the dying.
One: Bless these our gifts, O God, in the name of Jesus Christ, your blessing for us. Amen.

Commissioning

One: This is new life;
All: the old half-truths confronted.
One: This is new life;
All: a leap of freedom taken.
One: This is new life;
All: a hand stretched out through understanding, for friendship.
One: This is new life;
All: the Way of Jesus Christ risked.

A Blessing...

One: May the peace of Christ enfold you,
All: The love of God will secure us.
One: The Holy Spirit inspire you and those you love,
in our time and beyond all time. Amen.

Lent 3

Lectionary Readings
Exodus 17:1-7
Psalm 95
Romans 5:1-11
John 4:5-42

Call to Worship

One: God is for us and with us all the time.
All: We respond to our ever-present God with worship.
One: God's creative goodness goes way beyond our understanding.
All: We respond to our generous God with thanksgiving.
One: God calls us into faith community.
All: We respond to the God who unites us, with support and service.
One: God shows us the complex needs of our world.
All: We respond by bringing change gently, as we follow the life pattern of Jesus Christ.
One: God secures us when our world is threatening and uncertain.
All: We respond by helping others towards the security they seek.

Opening Prayer

One: Living Water: your gift, O God;
All: Living Water begins as a trickle, a few drops, the slightest suspicion of the Holy in the ordinary pattern of life.
One: Living Water: your inspiration, O God;
All: Living Water becomes a gentle stream; enlivening our worship, bringing us inspiration from the scriptures, calling us to reflection and to new endeavours.
One: Living Water: source of community, O God;
All: Living Water flows into the river; embracing us and other faithful people; showing us how much we can do when we link hands and hearts in the Way of Jesus Christ.
One: Living Water: refreshment of the saints, O God;

All: **Living Water becomes a part of the vast seas; joining us in solidarity, with persons of every age and faith and tradition; persons who worship the one Holy God. Amen.**

Prayer of Confession

One: O God, you recall our words, spoken in anger, spoken without thought.

All: **Give us the ability to speak the words that calm, and the attitude that encourages, and brings peace.**

One: O God, you are aware of friendships that are unhealthy, the relationships that lack trust.

All: **Give us the ability to understand the reasons for disharmony, and the willingness to bring change.**

One: O God, you know well the actions that have hurt, and those times when we have held back from support or care.

All: **Give us the courage to follow where our conscience leads, and the patience to persevere.**

One: O God, you feel our uncertain faith, and our lack of commitment to the Community of Jesus Christ;

All: **Give us the determination to learn and grow in faith, and to work with others to make clear the significance of Jesus for today.**

Time of silent reflection…

Words of Assurance

One: We look, O God, for signs that you are with us, for signs that we will be able to follow the faithful path in the coming days;

All: **and you point us to the heroes of Hebrew and Christian Scriptures, and the saints of the ages.**

One: You remind us of Moses in the desert, the prophet Jeremiah, Jesus going to Jerusalem, Paul in prison.

All: **You remind us of Saint Francis of Assisi, and John Newton; of Dietrich Bonhoeffer, and Martin Luther King.**

One: In the strength of the saints we have nothing to fear; you will go with us as you did with them.

All: **God's pardon and peace will be ours. Thanks be to God!**

Offering Prayer

One: We have received from you, O God, far beyond our understanding;
All: enable us to give with Christ-like generosity. Amen.

Commissioning

One: You bring us to our senses, Loving God;
All: Open our ears, O God; your Word will engage us.
Open our eyes, O God; your opportunities will be clear to us.
Enlighten our minds, O God; your purpose will be revealed to us.
Touch our hearts, O God; your compassion will be a part of us.
Infuse our spirits, O God; your loving Spirit will transform us.

Lent 4

Lectionary Readings
1 Samuel 16:1-13
Psalm 23
Ephesians 5:8-14
John 9:1-41

Call to Worship

One: Lead us gently as we worship, O God.
All: With you we have everything we need.
One: You give us calm in the midst of stress,
the light of hope when the world seems dark.
All: You strengthen and restore us.
One: You enable us to make the right choices,
and sustain us in the fearful times.
All: You are a good friend to us.
One: You, O God, are the source of a life that is
faithful and fulfilling;
All: as day follows day, as year follows year; all through life!

Opening Prayer

One: Children of the light, worship your God with joy!
**All: The gifts of each new day, the ties of family and friends,
bring us to God with thanksgiving.**
One: Children of the light, worship your God in community!
**All: The traditions of the church, the witness of wonderful saints,
bring us to God with thanksgiving.**
One: Children of the light, worship your God with just acts!
**All: The inclusion of those looked down upon, the acceptance of the
disadvantaged, bring us to God with thanksgiving.**
One: Children of the light, worship your God, known in Jesus Christ!
**All: Jesus' ministry of compassion and his sacrifice of the cross, bring
us to God with thanksgiving. Amen.**

A Prayer for Insight (Confession)

One: Open our eyes, O God,
All: and we will be able to see the gifts and talents in ourselves, which others can see.
One: Open our eyes, O God,
All: and we will enable others to see the gifts and talents in themselves, which we can see.
One: Open our eyes, O God,
All: and we will be able to see the powerless in our neighbourhoods, and stand beside them.
One: Open our eyes, O God,
All: and we will be able to see those struggling and fearful in our faith community, and give them compassionate support.
One: Open our eyes, O God,
All: and we will be able to see those in our world denied basic necessities and freedom, and understand their suffering.

Time of silent reflection...

Words of Assurance

One: We say, "we lack the personal skills that our situation requires."
All: God says, "believe in yourselves, and venture out in faith."
One: We say, "we do not have the time or the energy to make a difference."
All: God says, "in my strength you can take small steps, and bring change."
One: We say, "on our own we have such limited resources."
All: God says, "work with others in your faith community, and the outcome will surprise you."
One: We say, "will we know pardon and peace?"
All: God says, "persevere faithfully, and my peace will be yours."
One: Thanks be to God! Amen.

Offering Prayer

One: Gracious God, we offer this money as a way of serving you, and we offer ourselves as willing partners in that service.

All: Bless us as we go to work; bless the use of these gifts by the church, that you may be glorified in worship, that the questioning may receive answers, the suffering may receive help, and the way of Jesus may be honoured. Amen.

Commissioning

One: God will lead you as a shepherd leads his sheep.

All: God will lead us carefully; God knows each one of us by name.
God will lead us wisely; we have God's word on that.
God will lead us bravely; God knows our strength and limitations.
God will lead us in faith, and bring us back to the right paths.

One: You are God's flock. God will never let you down.

Lent 5

Lectionary Readings
Ezekiel 37:1-14
Psalm 130
Romans 8:6-11
John 11:1-45

Call to Worship

One: We move towards the City and the Cross;
All: uncertainty grips us, as it does the disciples.
One: We know that enthusiasm will turn to rejection;
All: what will it take to keep our commitment strong?
One: The powers of evil and self-serving are ready for us.
All: Will we have the courage to stay faithful?
One: The sacrifice of God's Loved One appears inevitable.
All: Are we ready to be worthy of the name, "Christian"?

Opening Prayer

One: We are a worshipping community, marked with the Cross.
All: We will "sing the praise of him who died."
One: We are a community of friends, marked with the Cross.
All: We will work together to defeat the forces of injustice.
One: We are a community of faith, marked with the Cross.
All: We will proclaim the Good News,
that nothing can withstand God's enlivening love.
One: We are a venturing community, marked with the Cross.
All: In our acceptance, in our readiness to serve, in our endurance, we will proclaim the root of our discipleship. Amen.

A Passion Prayer of Confidence (Confession)

One: Most loving and understanding God,
the jeering crowd no longer influences us.
All: We will speak out for the faithful way, even if it costs us.
One: The nails no longer have the last word.

All: We will break free from those situations that hold us fast.

One: The persuasive speech of a powerful leader no longer controls us.

All: We will trust in our own abilities and will look to the pattern of Jesus Christ.

One: The stress of suffering, the thought of dying, no longer dominates us.

All: We will face the most severe tests and win through.

Time of reflection…

Words of Assurance

One: You inspire us to freedom, O God.

All: The old patterns are overcome, new ways are followed,
confidence is restored.
You liberate us from dryness
and dead ends to find ourselves;
You free us to serve the powerless and oppressed.

One: Live in God's freedom, and know peace!

All: Thanks be to God! Amen.

Offering Prayer

One: With these gifts, O God, the
downhearted will be enlivened and
the suffering given hope.

All: With these gifts, the faith of young persons
will be nurtured, and those of advanced years strengthened.

One: With these gifts, O God, the inner-city powerless
will be given confidence, and the rural poor supported.

All: With these gifts, young adults overseas will find job training,
and abused women will find an affirming community.

One: Bless these gifts as they go to work, O God.

All: Through them, the name of Jesus will be honoured. Amen.

Commissioning

One: Bring us to life, O God;
All: free us from all the deadness of the past.
One: Bring us to life, O God;
All: free us to break through self-imposed limits.
One: Bring us to life, O God;
All: free us to give with abundant generosity.
One: Bring us to life, O God;
All: free us to follow Jesus faithfully.

Lent 6

Palm/Passion Sunday

Lectionary Readings for the Liturgy of the Palms

Matthew 21:1-11

Psalm 118:1-2, 19-29

Call to Worship

One: Gather with the crowds to await the coming of Jesus.

All: We have taken his words to heart; we are moved by his compassion.

One: Rejoice with the disciples, that God's Anointed One has courageously chosen to enter the city.

All: We recognize the evil forces Jesus will encounter; we will stand with him.

One: Cheer with the crowd, "Blessed is he who comes in God's name."

All: Blessed indeed! "God's Kingdom is close, Hosanna in the highest!"

Opening Prayer

One: We stand with the crowd, who welcomes God's Anointed One;

All: We rejoice in Jesus' courage, for we feel the threat of the religious and military powers.

One: We stand with the crowd, who welcomes God's Anointed One.

All: We rejoice that Jesus is with his friends, the disciples, but we wonder whether they can withstand the stress.

One: We stand with the crowd, who welcomes God's Anointed One.

All: We rejoice in the acceptance of the onlookers, of one so holy, but we ask ourselves, "can they resist the evil pressure of the leadership?"

One: We stand with the crowd, who welcomes God's Anointed One.

All: We rejoice that God's just and compassionate way has been recognized, but we wonder, will the love of God triumph in the coming crisis? Amen.

Prayer of Confession

One: On his last journey, the journey to Jerusalem, Jesus was acclaimed with joy.

All: When our worship lacks joy and enthusiasm, O God, forgive us.

One: On his last journey, the journey to Jerusalem, Jesus was encouraged by his disciples.

All: When our discipleship is faint-hearted and lacks staying power, O God, forgive us.

One: On his last journey, the journey to Jerusalem, Jesus was confronting evil and self-serving powers and groups.

All: When we compromise with evil, and seek to control the vulnerable and powerless, O God, forgive us.

Time of silence…

Words of Assurance

One: When all is going well, it is easy to support the way of Christ,
but when the tough times come, it is easy to walk away.

All: You are with us in the good days, O God, but you are also with us when we are tried and tested.
You are with us when we confess our lack of loyalty and trust.
You are with us as we confess our fear of the powerful ones.
You are with us as we renew our determination to take a stand with Jesus Christ.
You never leave us, and will never leave us in all eternity.

One: In Christ, you have a fresh start; pardon and peace are yours.

All: Thanks be to God! Amen.

Offering Prayer

One: Gifts: clothes strewn in his path, a carpet of palm branches; tokens of loyalty, tokens of enthusiasm.

All: These gifts: tokens of thanksgiving, tokens of commitment, instruments of compassion and service.

One: As you blessed your Holy One, O God, bless these gifts now,

All: for they are given in memory of Jesus. Amen.

Commissioning

One: Go from this church with the sound of hosannas ringing in your ears.

All: We will take heart; Jesus is honoured and accepted.

One: The palms are waved, the sights of celebration are around you.

All: We will rejoice; God's realm is on the way.

One: The disciples are in solidarity with Jesus.

All: We are determined to strengthen our faith community.

One: There is a cross on a hill in the distance.

All: At these happy times, we will not forget that the time of hard testing is never far away.

Lectionary Readings for the Liturgy of the Passion

Isaiah 50:4-9a
Psalm 31:9-16
Philippians 2:5-11
Matthew 26:14 – 27:66 or Matthew 27:11-54

Call to Worship

One: There is agony in the garden, and God feels the pain;

All: there is security in God's steadfast love.

One: There is betrayal by a good friend, and God feels the rejection;

All: there is security in God's steadfast love.

One: There is an unjust hearing and trial, and God feels the powerlessness;

All: there is security in God's steadfast love.

One: There is mockery by the soldiers, and God feels the humiliation;

All: there is security in God's steadfast love.

One: There is a cruel death on the cross, and God feels the darkness;

All: there is security in God's steadfast love.

Opening Prayer

One: Sit with Jesus and the disciples as they eat bread,
drink wine, and give thanks.

**All: We rejoice in the sense of community,
but we know the testing time is near.**

One: Come with Jesus and the disciples to the Gethsemane garden.

All: **We see how easily the disciples miss the agony of Jesus, but we wish we could support him.**

One: Join the crowd, as Pilate offers them the choice, "Jesus or Barabbas?"

All: **We cannot believe that the crowd is so easily swayed, that the evil ones can get the upper hand.**

One: Stand beneath the cross, and look up with disbelief at the crucified one.

All: **We feel this ultimate moment of horror, but we have faith that God's love will win through. Amen.**

A Confessional Prayer for Holy Week

One: Palms waved, joyful shouts, Jesus royally acclaimed!

All: **We confess our lack of faithful enthusiasm.**

One: A towel and basin taken, a need seen clearly, the disciples' feet washed by Jesus.

All: **We confess our reluctance to serve the needy.**

One: Jesus at prayer, deeply troubled, needing his friends with him.

All: **We confess we have missed the right place and the right time.**

One: Peter in the courtyard, his leader falsely accused, their friendship fervently denied.

All: **We confess we have not always stood up for the Way of Jesus.**

One: Jesus on the cross, deeply wounded, yet deeply forgiving.

All: **We confess we have been quick to judge, yet slow to forgive.**

Time of silent reflection…

Words of Assurance

One: When we hear the cry "Crucify him!"
when we ourselves cry "Crucify him!"
when the powerful ones of our day cry "Crucify him!"

All: **stay with us, O God;**
empower us to change, and give us that steadfastness,
that endurance, that strength of spirit,
that will prove our faithfulness,
even if it leads to our own cross. Amen.

Offering Prayer

One: What we offer to you, O God, has a cost:
in work carried out, in pensions shared, in money saved.

**All: What Jesus offered to us, has a cost: in joy
and a normal life passed up, and a criminal's cross at the end of it all.**

One: As we put these gifts to work, O God, keep us conscious of
the sacrificial price paid,

**All: and show us how to work out our thanksgiving,
as sharing members of this faith community. Amen.**

Commissioning

One: The gathered disciples around the Passover table

All: call us to give thanks, and to remember the sacrifice of Jesus.

One: The sleeping disciples in the garden

All: call us to be alert, and to watch for those who need our support.

One: The denial by Peter in the High Priest's courtyard

All: calls us to consider the strength of our faith, and to renew our loyalty.

One: The shouts of "Crucify him!" by the crowd

All: call us to think carefully about public opinion and the forces that have shaped it.

One: The cruel mocking by the soldiers

**All: calls us to think carefully about the power we possess,
and how we use it.**

One: The insults of the crucifixion crowd

All: call us to wonder at the way people can be influenced by evil.

One: The "no show" by the disciples

All: calls us to wonder at the effect of fear and its influence over good people.

Lent 7

Holy Thursday

Lectionary Readings
Exodus 12:1-4, (5-10), 11-14
Psalm 116:1-2, 12-19
1 Corinthians 11:23-26
John 13:1-17, 31b-35

Call to Worship

One: What can we offer to God, for all God's goodness?
All: We can offer a spirit of careful listening to God's Word.
One: What can we offer to God, for all God's goodness?
All: We can offer an openness to new insights for our day and situation.
One: What can we offer to God, for all God's goodness?
All: We can offer a willingness to participate with others in faithful work.
One: What can we offer to God, for all God's goodness?
All: We can offer a readiness to serve those excluded from prosperity, who have little and need much.

Opening Prayer

One: We are ready to serve as Jesus served,
All: those closest to us: family and friends.
One: Our service reaches out, as the service of Jesus did,
All: to touch the powerless, those deemed to be worthless, and troublemakers.
One: It is hard to make the sacrifices we need, to meet crying needs;
All: yet we have a pattern before us, of Jesus the Compassionate One.
One: He went out of his way to identify those poor in resources, and poor in spirit;
All: and the strength of our discipleship is tested by his example. Amen.

Prayer of Confession

One: The love of Jesus was constant and enduring.

All: There are persons who we find difficult to put up with, let alone love.

One: The love of Jesus was insightful, careful, and without discrimination.

All: There are persons who by reason of their personality, or our prejudice, we avoid.

One: The love of Jesus was practical and focused on suffering individuals.

All: We are skilled at avoiding a response, quick to rationalize our inaction.

One: The love of Jesus cost him his life on the cross.

All: We look up at the suffering and sacrifice, and begin to understand what loyalty might mean to us.

Time of silence…

Words of Assurance

One: With bowl and with towel Jesus signified his call to the disciples to serve;

All: He calls us to do the same.

One: Are you ready for the task of identifying need and serving faithfully?

All: We are ready!

One: Then get to work; God's peace will be your peace; God's pardon will be yours.

All: Thanks be to God! Amen.

Offering Prayer

One: Bless, O God, all we have given in the service of Christ,
and bless these gifts as tokens of our continuing wish to serve.

All: Through them the hungry will be fed, the suffering will be supported, the exploited will have their eyes opened, and the Good News will be preached.

One: And the name of Jesus Christ will be honoured.

All: God be praised! Amen.

Commissioning

One: Go from this church, as servants of the Blessed One.

All: We will not cease from doing good!

One: Will you stand beside the refugee?

All: We will.

One Will you give time to the depressed?

All: We will.

One: Will you look to the needs of your neighbourhood?

All: We will.

One: Will you participate with others in your faith community?

All: We will.

One: Will you give time and money, to help the downtrodden in this unjust world?

All: We will.

One: In all your service of others, will you keep
in mind the love and example of Jesus Christ ?

All: We will.

Lent 8
Good Friday

Lectionary Readings
Isaiah 52:13 – 53:12
Psalm 22
Hebrews 10:16-25
or Hebrews 4:14-16; 5:7-9
John 18:1 – 19:42

Call to Worship

One: Take us to Golgotha, O God, show us the maimed figure on the cross.

All: Show us a young woman, legs shattered by a land mine in Cambodia.

One: Take us to Golgotha, O God, show us the tortured figure on the cross.

All: Show us a young man led into drug addiction in our community.

One: Take us to Golgotha, O God, show us the abused figure on the cross.

All: Show us the face of a child molested by one she knows well.

One: Take us to Golgotha, O God, show us the frail figure on the cross.

All: Show us the old Jew scarred by the holocaust of humanity.

One: Take us to Golgotha, O God, show us the sorrowful figure on the cross.

All: Show us the young Jew whose face is etched with the agony of all humankind.

Opening Prayer (A Good Friday Meditation)
The Way to The Cross

One: A way in community; disciples gathered, bread and wine shared, solidarity of purpose, but the hint of betrayal.

All: The sense of all we share as a faith community gathered for worship; the sense of compassion and Christian action we share, when need is keenly felt.

One: A way of betrayal and denial; a trusted disciple turns Jesus over to the powerful ones, another denies all knowledge of him.

All: The unthinkable happens, friends turn disloyal, principles are compromised, evil triumphs over good.

One: A way where the powerful win out; an unjust trial, abusive leaders, torture and then the nails hammered in.

All: Misgiving, anxiety, and self-reproach, as we realize how often we compromise with the powerful ones, and turn a blind eye to community injustice.

One: A way that ends on the cross.

All: Dreams stilled in the reality of death, the potential for good overcome, evil wins out for the moment.

One: A way that does not end on the cross!

All: God be praised! Amen.

Prayer of Confession

One: Were you there? Encouraging, welcoming, applauding one moment, but shouting, "crucify him, crucify him!" the next.

All: We were there, we were there.

One: Were you there? Using your power over one at a disadvantage, unwilling to listen to your heart and your conscience, reluctant to let a good man go free.

All: We were there, we were there.

One: Were you there? Hammering in the nails, just doing your job; trying to isolate your feelings from your work, sensitive to your own lack of integrity.

All: We were there, we were there.

One: Were you there? Looking up and seeing someone you love suffer, but unable to help; wishing fervently that you had told this dear one that you loved him; recognizing his worth, yet not confident enough to declare it.

All: We were there, we were there.

Time of silent reflection…

Words of Assurance

One: You were not involved in the crucifixion of Jesus,

All: yet we are involved. We have avoided the issue, acted with hostility, judged unfairly, closed our eyes to the hurting ones, and have not stayed the course. We are sorry!

One: Crucifixion is not the last word; the light is breaking over the hillside, the followers are regaining their resolution, peace is Christ's promise.

All: It is *not* finished, thanks be to God! Amen.

Offering Prayer

One: We hear the hammering, we look up and see the broken body, and find our gifts to be superficial and inadequate;

All: God receives more than our money.
God receives our willingness to serve those whom Jesus cared for: the poor, the powerless, the sick, the lonely, and the despairing.

One: Your gifts will help!

All: God be praised! Amen.

Commissioning

One: Go forth to serve the crucified Christ.

All: We will serve him as we comfort the dying;
we will serve him as we confront the powerful;
we will serve him as we stir up the apathetic;
we will serve him as we listen to the lonely;
we will serve him as we take the words of children seriously;
we will serve him as we heed the wisdom of the elders;
we will serve him as we accept the Way that leads to the cross.

One: Go in peace to serve the Crucified One.

Easter Sunday

Lectionary Readings
Acts 10:34-43 or Jeremiah 31:1-6
Psalm 118:1-2, 14-24
Colossians 3:1-4 or Acts 10:34-43
John 20:1-18 or Matthew 28:1-10

Call to Worship *(with joy!)*
One: Easter is here.
All: Alleluia!
One: Death is defeated.
All: Alleluia!
One: Hope is alive.
All: Alleluia!
One: Community is restored.
All: Alleluia!
One: Christ is risen.
All: He is risen indeed. Alleluia!

Opening Prayer
One: Christ is risen!
All: Worship comes alive, and resounds with joy and thanksgiving.
One: Christ is risen!
All: The lonely find friends, and join in caring community.
One: Christ is risen!
All: The dejected ones find peace, and celebrate enthusiastically.
One: Christ is risen!
All: Good News is proclaimed, and breaks down all barriers. Amen.

Prayer of Confession
One: We move from cruel cross to empty tomb;
All: the routines of life have deadened us, but we believe that joy and creativity lie ahead.
One: We move from testing cross to empty tomb;

All: **we have faced the harsh realities, but we believe that life will laugh and dance again.**

One: We move from evil cross to empty tomb;

All: **injustice is no longer acceptable to us, and we believe the powerful ones will be confronted.**

One: We move from hopeless cross to empty tomb;

All: **our faith has been marked by apathy, but we believe our spirits will sing as we go about Christ's saving work.**

Time of silence…

Assurance of Pardon

One: The stone has been rolled away; new life is before you.

All: **We are ready to deal openly with the past. We are ready to live joyfully in the present. We are ready to grasp an adventurous vision of the future.**

One: Pardon, peace, the risen life, is yours in Jesus Christ.

All: **Thanks be to God! Amen.**

Prayer of Dedication *(in unison)*

One: O God, through these gifts we proclaim new life in the risen Christ:

All: **a challenge to the uncaring,**
peace in the struggle to the suffering,
a renewed vision to the despairing,
the warmth of friendship to the lonely,
action to the apathetic,
justice to the downtrodden.

One: Bless these gifts, and our gifts of talent and time,
that used together within the faith community,
all may know that Jesus lives. Amen.

Commissioning

One: Risen with Christ, share your enthusiasm!

All: We will celebrate with the joyful,
we will comfort the sorrowing,
we will give confidence to the downhearted,
we will encourage the hope-starved,
we will bring faith to the doubting,
we will share resources with the needy human family.

One: And you will be wonderfully blessed!

2nd Sunday of Easter

Lectionary Readings
Acts 2:14a, 22-32
Psalm 16
1 Peter 1:3-9
John 20:19-31

Call to Worship

One: You meet us in our questioning,
All: yet encourage us to explore and express our doubts.
One: You meet us in our individual faith,
All: yet remain with us when faith grows and shares within community.
One: You meet us as we focus on local needs,
All: yet show us our vital part in service and in mission, beyond this locality.
One: You meet us as we come away from the cross-hill,
All: yet surprise us as we encounter the risen Jesus Christ.

Opening Prayer

One: There is joy in the upper room.
All: The old despair is gone; new life in Christ surprisingly appears.
One: There is challenge in the upper room.
All: The new realities are questioned; faith comes alive in the testing.
One: There is peace in the upper room.
All: The old anxieties are forgotten; a new enthusiasm is courageously evident.
One: There is Jesus Christ in the upper room.
All: The focus for change, the promise of life unending. Amen.

Prayer of Affirmation (Confession)

One: Christ lives! A challenge to cross-shattered hopes.

All: In Jesus, we will find the means to bring our dreams to reality.

One: Christ lives! A contrast to those who predict doom and destruction.

All: In Jesus, we will see the sun break through clouds of defeat and uncertainty.

One: Christ lives! A rock-steady marker in the shifting sands of life.

All: In Jesus, we will find the values that count, and the firm basis for a healthy faith community.

One: Christ lives! A strong token of your enduring love, O Most Gracious God.

All: In Jesus, the aspirations of leaders, prophets, and wise ones come together, and prove that your love is effective beyond measure.

Time of silence…

Words of Assurance

One: The tomb is empty!

All: The reasons for inaction are gone;
the fears that haunt us are dispelled;
the guilt of the past is worked through;
the ties of faith community are heartening and strong;
the needs of refugees, and those without rights in our world,
are seen as our concern.

One: You are rising to new life; pardon and peace are yours!

All: Thanks be to God! Amen.

The Doxology (in unison)

Christ is the head and cornerstone,
Christ's name is Love, his Way is known,
God raised our Christ to glorious light,
our Easter joy affirms God's might. Amen.

Offering Prayer

One: Raise us to life, O God!

All: With gifts that disclose generosity,
with gifts that bring us together,
with gifts that banish fear,
with gifts that show compassion,
with gifts that reflect the Christ.

One: Raise us to life, O God,

All: with these gifts, which bring Easter hope
in the risen Jesus Christ. Amen.

Commissioning

One: Create a faith community of hope;
serve a faith community of compassion;
work for a just faith community;
strive for a faith community that looks and works beyond its own walls.

All: We will nurture a faith community of mutual support and freedom-bringing;
we will rejoice in a faith community creating peace:
peace in the Risen Jesus Christ.

3rd Sunday of Easter

Lectionary Readings
Acts 2:14a, 36-41
Psalm 116:1-4, 12-19
1 Peter 1:17-23
Luke 24:13-25

Call to Worship

One: Join us on our journey, Living God;
All: we have feelings to express, experiences to share.
One: Walk with us on our journey, Compassionate God;
All: we have memories to recall, faith stories to tell.
One: Reveal yourself to us on the journey, Surprising God;
All: we have thanksgiving to offer, bread and wine to share and community to nurture.
One: Strengthen us for our own journeys, Ever-Present God;
All: we have commitment to pledge; we have Christ's work to do.

Opening Prayer

One: Your eternal presence, O God, takes our breath away.
Author of time, Creator of galaxies and Mother Earth, Creator of each child who is born;
All: your creation is vast and breathtaking, yet you sent Jesus, human and vulnerable, Jesus who died on a cross.
One: In the death of Jesus, evil was confronted and defeated,
but the friends of Jesus turned away;
All: The first Easter brought transformation. Death was defeated,
Jesus rose to change humanity for good,
and the disciples got their confidence back.
One: The risen spirit of Jesus, alive in today's faith communities,
brings food to the hungry, hope to the despairing, and support to the challenged.

All: For the living influence of Jesus, we praise and worship you, O God! The scope of Christian service, the joy of those who follow the way of Christ, and your love at the center of it all, takes our breath away. Amen.

Prayer of Confession

One: You surprise us along the highway of life, O God.

All: You make clear the ways that are destructive,
the attitudes that harm relationships, and the words that offend.

One: You surprise us as citizens of a small planet, O God.

All: You make clear practices that destroy fertile land and pure air,
you identify the carelessness that favors polluters, and the selfishness that favours the "haves" over the "have-nots."

One: You surprise us as members of the Christian family, O God.

All: You make clear those aspects of our common life that dishonor the name of Jesus Christ; our lack of vision, our narrow-mindedness, our apathy. You call on us to show the big-heartedness of Jesus.

Time of silent reflection…

Words of Assurance

One: God will break into our pattern of living.

All: God will infiltrate our most hardened ways, our most grooved attitudes, our most habitual responses.

One: Trust God, and change is inevitable; trust God,
and we are enabled to start afresh.

All: We are ready for a new phase of life!

One: Pardon and peace are yours.

All: Thanks be to God! Amen.

Offering Prayer

One: It is amazing how quickly the change-around will come,
if Christ is known to be among us!

All: The followers are inspired again,
the faith community comes together,
the Word is preached,
the needs of mind and body are met,
the downhearted are filled with hope,
the powerful are cut down to size.

One: And these gifts make change possible.

All: God will bless them. We give God thanks. Amen.

Commissioning

One: You travel along life's highway, and often it seems humdrum
and ordinary, even discouraging at times.

All: But then, God meets us along the road, and we feel
the joy of God's presence.

One: You experience God's love, and you come to
share God's love with family, friends,
and those you encounter day by day.

All: We feel our spirits restored, our purpose clarified,
and our faith in Jesus Christ affirmed.

4th Sunday of Easter

Lectionary Readings
Acts 2:42-47
Psalm 23
1 Peter 2:19-25
John 10:1-10

Call to Worship

One: Bring us together, O God, as a shepherd gathers the flock.
All: Your care for us is wholehearted.
One: Sustain us, O God, in the testing situations of life.
All: Your strength is our endurance.
One: Keep us faithful, O God, when we feel most alone.
All: Your friendship is expressed through your people.

Opening Prayer

One: Your Easter gift surprises us, O Loving God.
All: When we felt that death had the last word, Christ is among us.
One: Your Easter gift delights us, O Loving God.
All: When we put limits on our achievements and our happiness,
Christ is not bound by them.
One: Your Easter gift challenges us, O Loving God.
All: When we would keep our faith to ourselves,
Christ encourages us to venture out unafraid.
One: Your Easter gift humbles us, O Loving God.
All: When we glory in our work for you,
Christ shows us his hands and side.
One: The risen Christ is your Easter gift, O Loving God;
All: We join with all the saints. We give thanks and we rejoice! Amen.

A Prayer of Challenge *(following the reading)*

Acts 2: 42-47 ... a wonderful community of Christ

One: Listen to this story of the early church; as a Christian community are we faithful?

All: Do we study God's Word, participate in the fellowship, find assurance in prayer?

Time of silence...

One: Listen to this story of the early church; are we faithful?

All: Do we use our talents in God's service, do we share generously?

Time of silence...

One: Listen to this story of the early church; are we faithful?

All: Do we praise and thank God joyfully, do we pass on the Good News enthusiastically?

Time of silence...

Words of Assurance

One: Continue reflecting on your life within this community of Jesus Christ.

All: We believe we have much to learn, much to be thankful for, and much to strive for, as a fellowship of God's people.

One: In your resolve to be faithful, in your acceptance of new truth,
in your determination to progress in new ways,
God's peace is your peace.

All: Thanks be to God! Amen.

Offering Prayer

One: Your voice, O God, is calling us to action:

All: to speak out for the needy,
to affirm the seekers,
to comfort the distressed,
to encourage the downhearted,
to challenge the complacent.

One: These gifts enable your voice to be heard; bless them!

All: Amen.

Commissioning

One: Listen to the voice of Jesus Christ!

All: He is calling us by name,
calling us to give thanks,
convincing us to listen carefully,
challenging us to live justly,
rejoicing that we share worship and service
with other Christians,
promising us peace within the struggle,
assuring us life, life in all its fullness.

One: Listen to the voice of Jesus Christ.

5th Sunday of Easter

Lectionary Readings
Acts 7:55-60
Psalm 31:1-5, 15-16
1 Peter 2:2-10
John 14:1-14

Call to Worship

One: You can trust God;
All: in the moments of celebration, at the high points of life,
God is there, God celebrates.
One: You can trust God;
All: in the dark moments, at the low points of life,
God is there, God sustains.
One: You can trust God;
All: in the moments of doubt, when decisions fail you,
God is there, God clarifies.
One: You can trust God;
All: in the certainty of faith, when you are inspired,
God is there, God goes with you. Let us worship God!

Opening Prayer

One: Jesus is the way:
All: the challenging way discovered by the disciples,
the way made glorious by the saints, the way we follow.
One: Jesus is the truth:
All: the truth that has stood the test of time, the truth that has empowered and encouraged, the truth we make our own.
One: Jesus is the life:
All: the life that combines commitment with adventure,
the life that is wholly satisfying, the life we have chosen.
One: Jesus is the way, the truth, and the life.
All: We will be faithful disciples of Jesus Christ. Amen.

Prayer of Confession

One: When we are caught up in our own importance,
All: give us a vision of Peter, who was humbled in Pilate's courtyard.
One: When we are lacking in self-confidence,
**All: give us a vision of the disciples in the Upper Room,
revived when Jesus walked with them.**
One: When we will only see one point of view,
**All: give us a vision of Saul on the Damascus Road,
encountering Jesus, whose followers he persecuted.**
One: When our loyalty wavers,
**All: give us the courage of Stephen,
who knew Jesus with him when he was killed.**
Time of silent reflection…

Words of Assurance

One: A change in attitude, a change in perspective, a change from inaction, are all possible for those touched by the risen Christ.
All: We are ready for change!
One: The pardon and peace of Christ are yours!
All: Thanks be to God! Amen.

Offering Prayer

One: We bring you our hope at this Easter season, O God,
**All: that compassion will be encouraged, doubts faced,
young persons will be supported, the challenged and distressed upheld, and the saving work of Jesus continued.**
One: Bless these hope-filled gifts, O God, and enliven the spirit of our giving. Amen.

Commissioning

One: Believe in Jesus Christ!
All: Jesus has God's blessing upon him.
One: Follow Jesus Christ!
All: He calls us to risk and adventure.
One: Be challenged by Jesus Christ!
All: He inspires us to promote justice and sharing.
One: Be moved by the sacrifice of Jesus Christ!
All: The cross measures our willingness to accept faithful responsibility.

6th Sunday of Easter

Lectionary Readings

Acts 17:22-31
Psalm 66:8-20
1 Peter 3:13-22
John 14:15-21

Call to Worship

One: This is the day to honour mothers.
All: Celebrate with us, Loving God.
One: This is the day to give thanks for our parents and grandparents.
All: Celebrate with us, Caring God.
One: This is the day to remember our whole family.
All: Celebrate with us, God of Fellowship.
One: This is the day to rejoice in our church.
All: Celebrate with us, Faithful God.
One: This is the day to recall the whole human family.
All: Celebrate a sharing world, Universal God.

Opening Prayer

One: With the loving vulnerability of a tiny baby,
All: we open ourselves to you, O God.
One: With the infinite curiosity of a growing child,
All: we search for you, O God.
One: With the joyful responsibility of young parents,
All: we rely on you, O God.
One: With the reflective experience of maturity,
All: we sense your presence, O God.
One: With the creaking wisdom of advancing years,
All: we rest in a hope strong and secure.
In our living, in our forgiving, in our loss and in our dying,
we look to you, O Eternally Present One.

A Family Prayer of Faith (Confession)

One: In the midst of conflict, uncertainty and unexpected loss,

All: **you offer us a confidence that endures, O God.**
One: In the midst of suffering, family stress, and broken promises,
All: **you offer us a love that endures, O God.**
One: In the midst of temptation, fear, and frustrated ambition,
All: **you offer us a hope that endures, O God.**
One: In the midst of self-pity, self-serving, and ignorance of another's need,
All: **you offer us the selfless Way of Jesus Christ, O God.**

Time of silence…

Assurance of Pardon (Christian Family Sunday)

One: God's love for families and God's compassion
is experienced in the testing situations of family life.
All: **We recognize God's compassionate love alive within the family circle. We want to be those persons in whom God's love is found, and through whom that love is expressed.**
One: God will grant you peace in your own time of trouble, and the ability to bring peace to others.
All: **Thanks be to God! Amen.**

Offering Prayer

One: Wherever we are, O God – home, church, work, friendship group, you go with us.
All: **You encourage us to discover ways to use all our gifts, and when we have decided, you inspire us to work diligently to help the suffering and despairing ones.**
One: Our gifts will receive a blessing, and be a blessing to many;
All: **for they belong to you, our Gracious God. Amen.**

Commissioning and Blessing

One: The blessing of God, Source of Love, Creator of families,
rest within your family.
All: **The blessing of Jesus Christ,**
acceptor of least as well as greatest,
bringer of peace, securer of hope, will
encourage our family living.
One: The blessing of the Holy Spirit,
inspiration to the downhearted, eternal worker for good, will
bring joy and challenge to your family.
All: **God be praised!**

7th Sunday of Easter

Lectionary Readings
Acts 1:6-14
Psalm 68:1-10, 32-35
1 Peter 4:12-14, 5:6-11
John 17:1-11

Call to Worship (inspired by Psalm 68)

One: Praise God!
All: God is eternally with us,
and worthy of our praise.
One: Praise God!
All: God, the author of change for good,
cares for the vulnerable,
brings friendship to the lonely,
creates freedom for the restricted,
and is hope for the poor and despairing.
One: Praise God!
All: God is universal, God is powerful, God is empowering;
therefore, with hearts and minds and spirits, we will praise God!

Opening Prayer

One: Reveal your presence with us, O God.
All: You are with us as we join in heartfelt praise.
One: Come close to us, O God.
All: You come close as we express our thanks and hopes in prayer.
One: Stay with us, O God.
All: You stay with us as we find courage in the testing times.
One: Inspire us for good, O God.
All: Your inspiration frees us to work for justice and for peace. Amen.

Prayer of Confession (based on the Hymn "Christ is Made the Sure Foundation")

One: "Christ is made the sure foundation."

**All: When we put our trust in money, popularity, or influence,
O God, give us fresh insight.**

One: "Christ the head and cornerstone."

**All: When we fail to take the words or spirit of Christ seriously,
O God, inspire us.**

One: "Christ binds all the church in one."

**All: When our faith is solitary, when our friendship is half-hearted,
O God, bring us to community.**

One: "One in glory, while unending ages run."

All: When we fear the trials of life, or the fact of death, O God, give us a new vision.

Time of silent confession…

Assurance of Pardon

One: God, we will bring the dark areas of our life into the light of your love; it will make a difference.

All: You give to us, O Most Loving God, the insight that leads to change, and the courage to make a fresh start.

One: Pardon and peace are yours.

All: Thanks be to God! Amen.

Offering Prayer

One: Through our discipleship, glory comes to you, O God.

**All: We offer you the love of our hearts;
we offer you the creativity of our minds;
we offer you the compassionate work of our hands;
we offer you the devotion of our spirits;
we offer you all we do as a church together.**

One: These gifts are a symbol of our faithfulness;

All: bless them, use them, and use our best talents with them, O God, that your name may be glorified in all the world. Amen.

Commissioning

One: As we go about our life we give glory to you, O God.

All: Glory for your presence in creation,
glory for your inspiration in the chores of each day,
glory for your spirit among our friends,
glory for your voice heard in the family,
glory for your call to help the nameless ones,
glory for our Christian heritage.

One: Keep us ever thankful.

All: Keep us ever joyful!

Pentecost Sunday

Lectionary Readings
Acts 2:1-21 or Numbers 11:24-30
Psalm 104:24-34, 35b
1 Corinthians 12:3b-13 or Acts 2:1-21
John 20:19-23 or John 7:37-39

Call to Worship

One: A breath in the stillness.
All: *(whisper)*...the breath of God surprisingly stirs within us.
One: A breeze to sway the treetops.
All: *(quietly)*...the Spirit of God brings us together to strengthen the faith community.
One: The strong wind sends the clouds flying.
All: *(louder)*...the Holy Spirit sends us out with the strength of Christian justice; and the compassion of Christ's love.
One: The force of the gale leaves nothing untouched, changing everything.
All: *(very loudly)*...with awe and wonder we rejoice, for God's realm is approaching.

Opening Prayer

One: We are people of God's Spirit;
All: we are different in personality, in background, in age, and in status, but we worship as one.
One: We are people of God's Spirit;
All: we have different needs, different fears, different hopes, but we know that God is here for us.
One: We are people of God's Spirit;
All: we are aware of crying injustice, unequal wealth, and loneliness, but we are determined to be God's co-workers for good.
One: We are people of God's Spirit;
All: we are different in faith, in church background, in our spiritual lives, but we find inspiration in Jesus, the Holy One. Amen.

A Prayer of Pentecostal Involvement

One: The Spirit moves! The horror of war crimes is revealed, the extent of poverty in this country is made clear, and the effect of addictions comes home to us.

All: When we get involved in international protest, work for better housing and support for the poorest, when we help friends set out on a healthy path, we know the freeing influence of God's Spirit.

One: The Spirit moves! The loneliness of persons in residential care becomes clear, the struggle of those with chronic illness is revealed to us, and we are aware of that empty place which is bereavement.

All: When we volunteer our time, patiently stay beside the sick, and are there for those who have lost loved ones, we know the compassionate influence of God's Spirit.

One: The Spirit moves! The need to make a decision is evident to us, the will to be reconciled with another stirs within us, the desire to confront our fear becomes real for us.

All: When we feel confidence growing within us, when we extend the hand of friendship, and find the courage to say heartfelt words, we know the energizing influence of God's Spirit.

Time of reflection...

Assurance of New Life

One: We thank you, O God, that you stand ready to bring renewal through the power of your Holy Spirit.

All: We believe you will grant us new insights, fresh resolve, and the peace that passes all understanding.

One: The peace of God is yours.

All: Thanks to be to God! Amen.

Prayer of Dedication

One: These gifts, O God, will work in partnership with your Spirit:
All: bringing old and young together in worship,
building faith community,
searching out the confused and lost,
restoring the sick and depressed,
reaching far beyond the shores of this nation, in practical help,
giving hope to those in the empty places of life.
One: Bless these gifts, O God, and influence them with your love.
All: We pray in the name of Jesus, your Beloved One. Amen.

Commissioning

One: In the power of the Holy Spirit, nothing is impossible!
All: We will leave the past behind carefully;
we will share generously;
we will face decisions bravely;
we will participate gladly;
we will confront evil without fear;
we will venture confidently;
we will be reconciled joyfully;
we will grasp discipleship enthusiastically.
One: With the Spirit you can find fulfillment, and live faithfully!

Trinity Sunday

First Sunday after Pentecost

Lectionary Readings

Genesis 1:1 – 2:4a
Psalm 8
2 Corinthians 13:11–13
Matthew 28:16–20

Call to Worship (adapted from Psalm 8)

One: "You have made us a little lower than the angels, O God."

All: We gather with all the saints of all the ages, to bring you joyful praise, Glorious God, Wonderful Creator.

One: "You have made us a little lower than the angels, O God."

All: We gather to give thanks for your Holy One, Jesus, our Saviour, our Teacher, and our Friend.

One: "You have made us a little lower than the angels, O God."

All: We gather under the influence of your Holy Spirit, to act justly, to love kindness, and to walk as your humble people.

Opening Prayer

One: Gracious God, whom we have come to understand in your Chosen One, Jesus, we worship you!

All: Jesus has given us the pattern of commitment, the Way to follow, and the cross-death to challenge us.

One: Loving God, source of everything we have, compassionate and ever-present, we worship you!

All: We have experienced wonderful creation, your willingness to endure with your people, and your gift of a Saviour.

One: Holy Spirit, who binds us together in fellowship and inspires us day after day, we worship you!

All: You give us joy and service within the faith community, and you work with us to build a better neighbourhood and world. Amen.

A Prayer for Discipleship

One: You know the challenge so well: "Go out, and encourage people everywhere to be disciples of Jesus Christ!"

All: We have heard the challenge, but help us, O God, to understand the nature of discipleship.

One: A disciple is ready to learn about the life and the teachings, the death and the rising, of Jesus the Christ.

All: We are ready to learn and to apply the teachings of Jesus; we know he confronts evil in his death, and gives us eternal hope in his rising to new life.

One: A disciple is always a member of a faith community. She or he works with others for good.

All: We enjoy our participation in the life of the church. Here we find friends, and are supported by others; from here we can go out to change our neighbourhood, and our world.

One: A disciple stands in awe of the love Jesus shared with his friends, the poor of the world, and those most despised.

All: We want to make that powerful love our own, and to welcome many more into the Community of the Baptized.

Time of reflection…

Words of Assurance

One: To be a disciple of Jesus Christ is a wonderful calling!

All: We have fallen short of our commitment as followers of Jesus, but we are ready to make a fresh start.
We will rededicate ourselves to learning;
we will rededicate ourselves to sharing in community;
we will rededicate ourselves to serving the downtrodden.

One: Do this, and God's pardon and peace will be yours.

All: Thanks be to God! Amen.

Offering Prayer

One: If the word and work of Jesus Christ are to be effective,
you must have resources to venture out.

All: It is through these gifts, O God, that we are enabled to share the life of Jesus for our time.
Through them, the compassionate word is heard;
through them, those who mourn are comforted;
through them, the despairing receive hope;
through them, the hungry are fed.

One: God's blessing is for these gifts, and goes with them
into the world.

All: To God be the praise and glory! Amen.

Commissioning

One: Go from this church in the power of the Holy Spirit!

All: Bring comfort to the sorrowing;
strengthen the fainthearted;
bring direction to the lost;
hear the deepest feelings of the depressed;
find the security of family;
rejoice in your friendships;
participate in community;
believe you can change a small corner of the world;
work faithfully always.

One: In the strength of the Spirit,
nothing is impossible!
Go in peace!

Sunday between May 29 & June 4 inclusive

Proper 4 [9] (if after Trinity Sunday)

Lectionary Readings

Genesis 6:9-22, 7:24, 8:14-19
Psalm 46
or
Deuteronomy 11:18-21, 26-28
Psalm 31:1-5, 19-24

Romans 1:16-17, 3:22b-28, (29-31)
Matthew 7:21-29

Call to Worship (Psalm 46, adapted)

One: Be still, know that God is here.
All: The mountains may rock, the waters may rage, God will not be moved!
One: Be still, know that God is here.
All: Governments may fall, rulers may be overthrown, God will not be moved!
One: Be still, know that God is here.
All: The terrorists may do their worst, civilization may hang in the balance, God will not be moved!

Opening Prayer

One: When the world is in turmoil and uncertainty prevails,
All: you, O God, call us to a steady faithfulness.
One: When the church is rocked with controversy, and conflict rages,
All: you, O God, call us to a quiet discernment.
One: When our family is tormented by quarrels, and anger reigns,
All: you, O God, call us to careful listening, and the task of reconciliation.

One: When our own life is troubled, and our Christian path is rough,
All: you, O God, call us to overcome apathy, and take action to bring change, as Jesus did. Amen.

Prayer of Assertion (Confession)

One: You ask that we lay down strong foundations for our life in Christ, O God;
All: you show us your Word, with all its wisdom of the ages.
One: You ask that we lay down strong foundations, O God;
All: you remind us of your saints, and challenge us to examine their values.
One: You ask that we lay down strong foundations, O God;
All: you call us to remember the faith community that nurtures us, and rejoice in its service.
One: you ask that we lay down strong foundations, O God;
All: you direct us to the Crucified and Risen One, and recall us to discipleship.

Time of reflection…

Words of Assurance

One: Your foundations will be rocked and shaken,
but in God's strength you will be secure!
All: We will recall the ground on which we stand:
Holy Ground, Gospel Ground, faithfully prepared,
and we will not be afraid.
One: You will know peace in the storms of life.
All: Thanks be to God! Amen.

Offering Prayer

One: What we give, O God, provides the means of security
to the suffering and depressed;
All: calm in the storms of life,
hope in the darkest moments,
a touch when words fail,
a word to open the flood gates of feeling,
a silence to stem the flow of words,

a wide perspective when the focus is, "me, here and now,"
a lively concern for the oppressed of every land.

One: Bless these offerings, O God;
given with care, they will make a difference. Amen.

Commissioning

One: You will be strong!

All: In the midst of life's storms, God is the rock.

One: You will be secure!

All: When other people's troubles come home to us, God is there.

One: You will be unafraid!

All: As we are battered by trials and temptations, God stands fast.

One: You will withstand the test!

All: Nothing, nothing in all creation, can separate us from the love of God.

Sunday between June 5 & 11 inclusive

Proper 5 [10] (If after Trinity Sunday)

Lectionary Readings

Genesis 12:1-9
Psalm 33:1-12
or
Hosea 5:15 – 6:6
Psalm 50:7-15

Romans 4:13-25
Matthew 9:9-13, 18-26

Call to Worship

One: Hearts and minds on fire; enthusiastically, joyfully, worship begins.
All: Cast down, sorrowing; feeling the darkness in our souls, worship begins.
One: Reluctantly, slowly, still engaged in the busyness of home; unprepared, worship begins.
All: Alert, hopeful, prayer-prepared, having confidence in Jesus, worship begins.
One: However we come before God, God accepts us, God welcomes us, God invites us to worship.
All: We are here, God is here, love is shared among us, we will worship God!

Opening Prayer

One: This is God's place and ours;
All: the place of worship, the place of praising, the place of learning, the place of searching.
One: This is God's community and ours;
All: the community of the covenant, the community of faith, the community of encouragement, the community of selfless service, the community whose common bond is Jesus Christ.

One: This is God's Word and ours;

All: the word of life; the word that inspires, the word that delights, the word that challenges.

One: We are your people, O Loving God;

All: a people of faith; children bubbling over with joy and questions, parents searching for answers, young persons setting out on their faith journey, wise elders sharing their wisdom. Amen.

Prayer of Confession

One: You call us to discipleship: to face the temptations, to listen to the voice of truth, to give of our talents wholeheartedly.

All: We will go so far, but will we go further?

One: You call us to the journey of faith: to search out the lost, to commit to the needy, to support the powerless, to grow in the compassion of Christ.

All: We will go so far, but will we go further?

One: You call us to the faith community, to the church: to worship with joy, to be there for each other, to work joyfully for the Way of Jesus Christ.

All: We will go so far, but will we go further?

One: You call us to renew ourselves: to learn and grow in the faith, to reflect carefully, to risk new directions, and to squarely face past wrongs.

All: We will go so far, but will we go further?

Time of silent reflection…

Words of Assurance

One: Hearing your call, O God, requires patience and concentration.

All: Responding to your call, O God, leads us to confession and repentance; it leads us to go further along the way of Christ.

One: With these insights, pardon and peace are yours.

All: Thanks be to God! Amen.

Offering Prayer

One: The gifts that Jesus offered to those around him
were generous and according to need;
**All: Jesus offered healing,
Jesus offered acceptance,
Jesus offered empowerment,
Jesus offered sight and insight,
Jesus offered the hopeful word,
Jesus offered comfort and a blessing.
We offer our gifts for blessing,
and we offer action in the week ahead.**
One: God goes to work with these gifts.
All: Thanks be to God! Amen.

Commissioning

One: Go from this church, as those who bring an end to fear.
**All: We will look out for the despised,
bring dignity to the disheartened,
see the worth of those who lack confidence,
take time with the depressed,
encourage the struggling,
confront the powerful,
celebrate with the liberated,
take the doom-sayers to task.**
One: Christ goes with you, a companion to those who are afraid.

Sunday between June 12 &18 inclusive

Proper 6 [11] (If after Trinity Sunday)

Lectionary Readings
Genesis 18:1-15 (21:1-7)
Psalm 116:1-2 12-19
or
Exodus 19:2-8a
Psalm 100

Romans 5:1-8
Matthew 9:35 – 10:8 (9-23)

Call to Worship (inspired by Psalm 116)

One: We come together because we love God;
All: we love God, because God is there for us all the time.
One: God is there for us when we prayerfully reach out;
All: God is there for us when trouble hits unexpectedly.
One: It is not only these gathered people whom God loves;
God embraces the poor, the powerless, and the rejected;
All: and God is there for us when our confidence crumbles, and when it seems that the whole world is against us.
One: Why God should care for us is beyond our understanding;
All: but God's gracious love has held us fast in the community of the faithful, and will endure from age to age.

Opening Prayer

One: O God, Wonderful Creator, we call you "Friend."
All: Like a good friend, you give your abundant gifts freely, and ask only loyalty in return.
One: O God, founder of the faith community, we call you "Friend."
All: Like a trusted friend, you listen carefully to your people, and support them in testing times.

One: O God, inspiration of the faith community, we call you "Friend."

All: Like a challenging friend, you encourage your people, and send them out to serve the powerless and needy ones.

One: O God, you graced us with Jesus your Chosen One;
we call you "Friend."

All: Like a faithful friend, Jesus came among us to bring acceptance, healing, and peace.
Thank you, Eternal Friend. Amen.

Prayer of Affirmation (Confession)

One: "Is anything too wonderful for God?"

All: That we might use the talents we have kept hidden,
and encourage the talents of others.

One: "Is there anything too wonderful for God?"

All: That we might affect the long sought reconciliation,
and face the deepest fear.

One: "Is there anything too wonderful for God?"

All: That our faith community might break from the groove of past practice, and engage in creative new ventures.

One: "Is there anything too wonderful for God?"

All: That we might accept a faithful pattern of discipleship;
confronting the greedy, and inspiring the dispirited,
in the Jesus way.

Time of reflection…

Words of Assurance

One: You will surprise yourselves by what you can achieve
in God's strength!

All: We are ready to trust God to strengthen us, and to lead us into new and faithful ventures.

One: Your past failures you can leave in the past; you will begin a new chapter with the peace of God for you, and with you.

All: Our discipleship will be breaking fresh ground. Thanks be to God! Amen.

Offering Prayer

One: These gifts will be blessed, as they are used to do God's work.
All: Children will sing joyfully of God's creation,
those of advanced years will laugh and reminisce,
young moms and dads will get together,
and the addicted and lonely will find a place to share.
One: The bible will be opened to the curious,
and the tuneful will raise the roof with their singing.
All: God's "work," will not seem like work at all.
Thanks be to God! Amen.

Commissioning

One: We go from here a hopeful people, for God goes with us.
All: In times of trouble, God will support us;
in times of weakness, God will be our strength;
in times of doubt, God will give us direction;
in times of loneliness, God will touch us with the friendship of others;
in times when we lack confidence, God will show us our worth;
in times of sadness, God will embrace us with love.
One: Nothing can dash your hopes!
All: In the power and the love of God, Amen.

Sunday between June 19 & 25 inclusive

Proper 7 [12]

Lectionary Readings
Genesis 21:8-21
Psalm 86:1-10 16-17
or
Jeremiah 20:7-13
Psalm 69:7-10 (11-15), 16-18

Romans 6:1b-11
Matthew 10:24-39

Call to Worship

One: You are with us, O God, whatever happens;
All: in the storms of life, when we do not know where to turn, you are there.
One: You are with us, O God, whatever happens;
All: in the wonderful days, when life dances and sings, you are there.
One: You are with us, O God, whatever happens;
All: as we make the choice that reflects our Christian calling, you are there.
One: You are with us, O God, whatever happens;
All: in the community of faith, as we worship and risk with others, you are there.
Whatever happens, you are with us, O Most Caring God!

Opening Prayer

One: There is new life in Jesus Christ, as there was new life for Peter;
All: an end to fishing on the lake, a beginning to changing others, and discovering his own limits.
One: There is new life in Jesus Christ, as there was new life for Mary Magdalene;

All: an end to searching for a purpose, a beginning to finding acceptance, and knowing her true friend.

One: There is new life in Jesus Christ, as there was for Matthew the tax-gatherer;

All: an end to the taking advantage of others,
a beginning to the sharing of love in community.

One: There is new life in Jesus Christ, as there was for Saul of Tarsus;

All: an end to attacking Christians, a beginning to an adventure with Christ, and mission to a hostile world.

One: There is new life in Jesus Christ, new life for each of us.

All: Thanks be to God. Amen.

Prayer of Confession.

One: We confess to you, O God, the anxieties that cloud our days:

All: concerns about family and friends, worries about work,
and a lack of confidence in our own abilities.

One: We confess to you, O God, the anxieties that cloud our church:

All: concerns about the health of faith community members,
questions about the direction of church life, and different opinions about how to follow Jesus.

One: We confess to you, O God, the anxieties that cloud our world:

All: concerns about the injustice between have and have-not nations,
worries about terror from outside and within,
and a lack of confidence in leaders' abilities to achieve a lasting peace.

Time of reflection…

Words of Assurance

One: If you believe that God is for you, if God who cares for the smallest bird, loves you beyond all reckoning, your worries and anxieties do not stand a chance.

All: We will bring our concerns before you, O God, and they will loose their grip on us;
our fear will drop away, and we will know peace.

One: The sense of calm in our soul,

All: **and that active peace which compels us to take steps to bring change, in our own life, in our church, and for our world.**

One: Peace and a fresh resolution are yours!

All: **Thanks be to God! Amen.**

Offering Prayer

One: Open our hearts, O God, in thanksgiving for all your many blessings.

All: **We present our gifts to help those who are suffering and downtrodden in this neighborhood and in other parts of the nation and world. With them we present our willingness to be partners in the work your Holy Spirit will accomplish with them.**

One: Your gifts will accomplish more than you could ever imagine.

All: **God be praised! Amen.**

Commissioning

One: Soar with the birds, have done with anxiety!

All: **We will leave our worries behind us.**

One: Reach for the clouds, dismiss your fears!

All: **We will replace our fears with opportunities.**

One: Fly beyond the limits, forget your failures!

All: **We will use our failures as stepping stones to success.**

One: Rise to the skies, have done with self-doubt!

All: **Confident and assured, we will go about Christ's work.**

Sunday between June 26 & July 2 inclusive

Proper 8 [13]

Lectionary Readings

Genesis 22:1-14
Psalm13
or
Jeremiah 28:5-9
Psalm 89:1-4, 15-18

Romans 6:12-23
Matthew 10:40-42

Call to Worship (Genesis 22:14)

One: For the joy and inspiration of worship,
All: "the Lord will provide."
One: For the deepening of faith within this community of Christians,
All: "the Lord will provide."
One: For the strength to endure the hard places of life,
All: "the Lord will provide."
One: For the courage to face the unknown future,
All: "the Lord will provide."
Let us worship God!

Opening Prayer

One: You accept and bless us, O God;
All: we know this, for you have given us a good earth, and the opportunity to live peacefully here.
One: You accept and bless us, O God;
All: for you have placed us in families and with friends, to know the experience of your love.
One: You accept and bless us, O God;

All: **this is our certainty, for you have given us the church in which to worship and to serve.**

One: You accept and bless us, O God;

All: **for you sent Jesus amongst us, your pattern of compassion, and sign of salvation.**

Prayer of Confession

One: Merciful God, we come humbly before you.

All: **We confess we have fallen short of the life to which you inspire us. Your pattern of selflessness in Jesus is clear to us, dear to us, but we have often chosen to ignore it.**

One: In Jesus, we have seen what it is to follow the path of pilgrimage and adventure,

All: **but so often we are insecure, and live by what we know.**

One: In Jesus, we have seen what it is to get to know some very different people, surprising people, challenging people.

All: **So often we stay with family, friends, and those familiar over the years.**

One: In Jesus, we have seen what it means to stand with the poor, the disadvantaged, and those who feel lonely;

All: **we find it hard to stand with those who experience life as a struggle, or who are depressed.**

One: In Jesus we have seen what it means to resist temptation, obvious and subtle;

All: **we confess we have given in.**

Time of reflection…

Words of Assurance

One: You need fresh courage and determination to live up to your calling as followers of Jesus Christ;

All: **we will find courage and determination as we look to the life of God's Anointed One, and pray and work in his spirit. We will find courage and determination as we draw strength from the members of the faith community, and share their experience.**

One: In Christ and Christ's church, pardon and peace will be yours.

All: **Thanks be to God! Amen.**

Offering Prayer

One: As mothers brought their children to Jesus, confident of a blessing, so we bring our gifts confident they will be blessed.

All: You will accept them, O God, you will use them, and in partnership with them, your community of people here, and far from here, will be a blessing. Amen.

Commissioning

One: Go from here a welcoming people!

All: We will welcome the newcomer to our church;
we will welcome the newcomer to our neighbourhood;
we will welcome the newcomer to our shores;
we will welcome those of whom we are suspicious;
we will welcome those who we take to our hearts;
we will welcome fresh realities;
we will welcome new ways;
we will welcome new hopes and dreams.

One: And God will bless you in your welcoming!

Sunday between July 3 & 9 inclusive

Proper 9[14]

Lectionary Readings

Genesis 24:34-38, 42-49, 58-67
Psalm 45:10-17 or Song of Solomon 2:8-13
or
Zechariah 9:9-12
Psalm 145:8-14

Romans 7:15-25a
Matthew 11:16-19, 25-30

Call to Worship

One: Hold us in your prayerful gaze, O God, as we come to worship;
All: we are your committed people, but we need your inspiration.
One: Remind us of your shadow over us, O God, as we come to worship;
All: you have gone with us in times past, but we need your reassuring presence.
One: Enable us to sense your love around us, O God, as we come to worship;
All: we are filled with thanksgiving, but there are testing times ahead.
One Enliven us through your Holy Spirit, O God, as we come to worship;
All: we are ready for action, but we need you to work within our faith community.

Opening Prayer

One: God, whose beauty is revealed in a summer rose,
All: we praise your creative perfection.
One: God, whose joy is revealed in the reunion of old friends,
All: we praise your never-failing companionship.
One: God, whose concern is revealed in the tough struggles,
All: We adore your essential peacefulness.
One: Be revealed in this time of worship, O God,

All: **as our voices sing your praise, as our minds are challenged by your Word, and as our hearts respond to your great love in Jesus, your Anointed One. Amen.**

Prayer of Confession

One: We mean well, O God, but often we do the wrong thing.

All: We are quick to give advice, but are slow to stop and listen.

One: We mean well, O God, but often we do the wrong thing.

All: We give a promise to another person, but then do not follow through.

One: We mean well, O God, but often we do the wrong thing.

All: We affirm our willingness to grow in the faith, but when the opportunity comes, we cannot find the time.

One: We mean well, O God, but often we do the wrong thing.

All: We pledge support to the faith community, but go it on our own.

One: We mean well, O God, but often we do the wrong thing.

All: We say we are "members of the family of all humankind," but fail to support those beyond the boundaries of our nation.

Time of reflection…

Words of Assurance

One: Jesus says, "come to me all you who are weary and carrying heavy burdens, and I will give you rest."

All: Jesus says, "take my yoke upon you, and you will find rest for your souls."

One: Jesus says, "For my yoke is easy and my burden is light." The peace of Christ is yours!

All: Thanks be to God. Amen.

Offering Prayer

One: O God, you have given to us beyond our wildest dreams,
and we are called to a thankful response.
All: Empower us, O God, to respond generously, wisely and compassionately,
that our gifts combined with the gifts of others,
may follow the pattern of Jesus Christ, and become a lively blessing. Amen.

Commissioning

One: Give us a child-like faith as we leave the church:
All: looking with awe at the billowing clouds,
and star-spread night sky;
celebrating the joy of each new day,
finding the deepest lessons in the simplest games,
ready to trust and share with friends,
prepared to forgive and start again,
wondering at the sheer goodness of Jesus,
believing totally in the love of our Heavenly Parent.
One: Go confidently in that love, for God goes with you.

Sunday between July 10 & 16 inclusive

Proper 10 [15]

Lectionary Readings
Genesis 25:19-34
Psalm 119:105-112
or
Isaiah 55:10-13
Psalm 65:(1-8) 9-13

Romans 8:1-11
Matthew13:1-9, 18-23

Call to Worship

One: We rejoice in God's presence!
All: Sensed on a sunlit day, reflected in the calm lake, God is with us.
One: We rejoice in God's presence!
All: Sensed in the hug of a child, reflected in the closeness of a couple long-married, God is with us.
One: We rejoice in God's presence!
All: Sensed in the faith community at prayer, reflected in an unnoticed caring act, God is with us.
One: We rejoice in God's presence!
All: Sensed in the living words of Jesus Christ, reflected in those through whom his Spirit moves, God is with us.

Opening Prayer

One: We are not here, O God, to be preoccupied with our own needs,
All: but to offer you our thanks and our praise.
One: We are not here, O God, to prove our own faithfulness,
All: but to think carefully about how we may proclaim the Good News.
One: We are not here, O God, to put right what cannot be changed,
All: but to reflect on the possibilities before us, for wholeness and healing.

One: We are not here, O God, to dwell on our own shortcomings,

All: but to remember your love for us in Jesus Christ, and to renew our discipleship. Amen.

A Prayer – Signs of God's Glorious Realm (Confession)

One: When God's Realm is a reality, disputes will be at an end, reconciliation a reality.

All: Keep us forgiving, O God; keep us compassionate and understanding of others.

One: When God's Realm is a reality, different opinions will be readily listened to, and the prejudice of race or gender will be forgotten.

All: Keep us open to new truth, O God; enable us to see the worth and wisdom of each person we meet.

One: When God's Realm is a reality, worship will come naturally and prayer will be a joyful experience.

All: Keep us learning and enthusiastic in our church life, O God, and enable us to share our faith naturally.

One: When God's Realm is a reality, the powerful ones will share their influence with the needy, and the hungry will be fed.

All: Keep us conscious of our resources and strength, O God, and give us the willingness to use our talents justly.

Time of reflection…

Words of Assurance

One: In Jesus Christ, self-centred ways are at an end, new opportunities are envisioned, and the will to bring change for good is found.

All: We are people of "the Way;" we will walk boldly with the example of Jesus before us, and the living spirit of Jesus with us.

One: Pardon and peace are yours.

All: Thanks be to God. Amen.

Offering Prayer

One: You have so gracefully shared your creation and your love for us, O God, and we respond with wholehearted thanksgiving.

**All: We thank you through our acts of worship;
we thank you as we carefully serve others;**

we thank you with these our gifts, given to sustain your faith community here, and to sustain faith communities far from here. Bless all our gifts, as you have blessed us in the gift of Jesus Christ. Amen.

Commissioning

One: God's generosity, given freely, given abundantly, amazes us.
We will share the spirit of generosity with those around us.

All: We will be ready to befriend the lonely.
We will be ready to help the downhearted.
We will take time to listen and understand.
We will proclaim the faith with boldness and with sensitivity.
We will act justly, love mercy, and walk humbly with our God.

The Parable of the Sower – A Pastoral Prayer

One: Jesus said, "A sower went out to sow, and as he sowed, some seeds fell on the path and others fell on rocky ground."
The continuing distrust between Israelis and Palestinians, the peace process at a standstill.

All: Rocky ground.

One: Those affected by the extremes of global climate; floods, forest fires, scorching heat.

All: Rocky ground.

One: Distrust between medical groups and government.

All: Rocky ground.

One: Loving God, may concern for future generations, efforts to bring help to those in tough situations, and an openness to the other person's point of view, bring forth a good harvest.
Illness which will not yield to treatment, waiting lists that are so long.

All: Rocky ground.

One: Troubled relationships for which there seems no resolution, no change.

All: Rocky ground.

One: The barren, empty place of bereavement.

All: Rocky ground.

One: Loving God, may a will to wholeness and healing
bring a harvest of peace. May the desire to begin again
bring a harvest of reconciliation, and the gentle comfort of friends
bring a harvest of hope.

The feeling of being stuck in circumstances that cannot be changed.

All: Rocky ground.

One: Fears hidden deep within us that cannot be released.

All: Rocky ground.

One: A faith life that is stale and unrewarding.

All: Rocky ground.

One: Loving God, may renewed determination bring a harvest
of new opportunity and new direction.
May a willingness to express our fears bring a harvest of freedom.
May a thorough exploration into the core of our faith bring
a joyful and spiritual harvest.

All: God of the good seed be praised! Amen.

Sunday between July 17 & 23 inclusive

Proper 11 [16]

Lectionary Readings
Genesis 28:10-19a
Psalm 139:1-12, 23-24
or
Wisdom of Solomon 12:13, 16-19 or Isaiah 44:6-8
Psalm 86:11-17

Romans 8:12-25
Matthew 13:24-30, 36-43

Call to Worship

One: God of each human family,
All: bless this church family, gathered in the name of Jesus.
One: God of each human family,
All: inspire this church family, gathered to praise your name, O God.
One: God of each human family,
All: challenge this church family, gathered to live by the Living Word.
One: God of each human family,
All: encourage this gathered church family to be good to each other, and to be movers and shakers in this neighbourhood.
One: God of each human family,
All: give a broad vision to this church family, gathered to serve the downtrodden of the world.

Prayer of Approach

One: You welcome us into your presence, O God,
All: as you have welcomed countless generations to this hour of worship.
One: You welcome us as those who take the Way of Jesus seriously.
All: May we be worthy of the Compassionate One from Nazareth.
One: You welcome us as friends in the church together;
All: give us grace to see the hidden gifts of each member, young or old.

One: You welcome us as those who are committed to change the world for good;

All: inspire us to make an impact in our small corner of this troubled planet. Amen.

Prayer of Confession (inspired by Psalm 139)

One: You have "searched us and known us," O God.

All: We try to lose you in the busyness of our day,
and in the variety of our interests, but you are there.

One: Even before we speak, you O God, know what we will say.

All: If only we would hold our tongue more often,
and listen to your voice, the voice of conscience!

One: We cannot get away from you, O God,
though there are times when we would like to!

All: You are there as we celebrate and rejoice,
but you are also there in our evasive and selfish moments.

One: You know our deepest thoughts and feelings, O God.

All: You give us the power to overcome the darkness
that clouds our thoughts and actions; you show us the eternally good way.

Time of reflection...

Words of Assurance

One: We struggle with the concepts of your eternal presence,
and your universal love, O God, yet we rejoice that in a world
shifting and changing, you are the rock, the one enduring reality.

All: And so we are able to trust you, when we stray from the right path,
to lead us to truth, and give us the will to follow
the compassionate Christian way again.

One: In following the pattern and example of Jesus Christ, sin is at an end.
God's peace is your peace!

All: Thanks be to God! Amen.

Offering Prayer

One: Your love, O God, in Jesus Christ, has blessed us, encouraged us, and given us hope. We respond with our offering.

All: Our offering will strengthen the church here, and the wider community of faith.
Through these gifts we will worship joyfully.
Through these gifts we will care compassionately.
Through these gifts we will provide hope globally,
and declare our faithfulness. Amen.

Commissioning

One: Take your responsibility as members of Christ's Church to heart!

All: We will study God's word diligently;
we will grow in the faith steadily;
we will serve our fellow men and women justly and carefully;
we will participate in the faith community enthusiastically;
and we will rejoice in what we share,
as those marked by the Cross of Jesus.

Sunday between July 24 & 30 inclusive

Proper 12 [17]

Lectionary Readings

Genesis 29:15-28
Psalm 105:1-11 45b or Psalm 128
or
1 Kings 3:5-12
Psalm 119:129-136

Romans 8:26-39
Matthew 13:31-33, 44-52

Call to Worship

One: O God, you have been with your people in times past.
All: Guiding Moses, instructing the prophets, finding your voice in Jesus, you have been the secure presence for all the generations before this one.
One: O God, you are with your people of this generation,
All: giving them purpose, inspiration, and faith community to share.
One: O God, you will be with your people in the generations that are to come:
All: providing a message of hope and certainty amid the shifting forces, and a love that will not let people go in time or in eternity.

Opening Prayer

One: When heaven comes on earth,
All: it will be because the smallest deeds have made an impact for good beyond our imagining.
One: When heaven comes on earth,
All: it will be because we know the most valuable source and search it out.
One: When heaven comes on earth,
All: it will be because we are ready to commit totally to God and God's Way.

One: When heaven comes on earth,
All: it will be because we recognize the loving influence of God, and the darkness that seeks to overcome it.
One: Each one of us has the opportunity,
All: to bring closer the Kingdom of Heaven. Amen.

Prayer of Confession

One: What can separate us from the love of Christ?
All: Can the darkness that clouds our days, the depression that gnaws away at our soul?
One: That won't do it! What can separate us from the Love of Christ?
All: Can the trust we place in the powers and institutions of this city, or this world?
One: That won't do it! What can separate us from the Love of Christ?
All: Can our refusal to face a broken friendship, or our need to make a decision?
One: That won't do it! What can separate us from the Love of Christ?
All: Can a lack of commitment to our local, or national faith community?
One: That won't do it! What can separate us from the Love of Christ?
All: Can a sense that "have" nations of the world should keep what is theirs, without sharing?
One: That won't do it! What can separate us from the Love of Christ?
All: Can the rejection of a refugee, can the suspicion of minority racial groups?
One: That won't do it! What can separate us from the Love of Christ?
All: Nothing in all creation can separate us from the Love of God, in Christ Jesus our Lord.

Time of reflection…

Words of Assurance

One: The love of God as we know it in Christ Jesus is an unsurpassed power for good.

All: To be aware of that power is to see our own faults and failings in perspective.

One: To be aware of that power is to see the way in which the church falls short of being a true community of faith.

All: The Holy Spirit will give us insight, will give us determination to begin afresh, and will renew our church.

One: The peace of Christ is yours!

All: Thanks be to God! Amen.

Offering Prayer

One: Our offering does not change everything; it is like the yeast in the dough: it is the means by which change begins to take place.

All: And so we offer our treasure, our talent, and our time to God, and patiently we wait for it to go to work for good.

One: God will receive what we bring, and in God's good time, we will notice the difference.

All: We trust that the blessing of God rests on these gifts. God's glory will be known through them. Amen.

Commissioning

One: The Kingdom of Heaven is worth working for!

All: The Kingdom will come, but only if we sow the good seed;
the Kingdom of Heaven will come, but only if we stop the evil that stifles;
the Kingdom of Heaven will come, but only if we recognize its worth, and work to bring it closer.
The Kingdom of Heaven will come, but only if we take ownership of its potential.

One: The Kingdom of Heaven will come, God will reign supreme,
and we will know and understand for the first and only time!

Sunday between July 31 & August 6 inclusive

Proper 13 [18]

Lectionary Readings
Genesis 32: 22-31
Psalm 17:1-7, 15
or
Isaiah 55:1-5
Psalm 145:8-9, 14-21

Romans 9:1-5
Matthew 14:13-21

Call to Worship

One: Truth is what we seek in our worship, O God;
All: Your truth never goes out of style.
One: Acceptance is what we search for in our worship, O God;
All: In Jesus you have made clear that each person is accepted.
One: Thanksgiving is what we bring in our worship, O God;
All: Our senses, our hearts rejoice in giving thanks.
One: Love is what we encounter in our worship, O God;
All: You have found us, held us, your love will never let us go.

Opening Prayer

One: This is where we long to be, O God:
All: praising you in the company of your faithful people.
One: This is what we need to hear, O God:
All: your timeless Word carefully read, fearlessly proclaimed.
One: This is how we are called to live, O God:
All: in the Way of Jesus, your Chosen One.
One: These are the ones we are challenged to serve, O God:
**All: men, women, and children, abused and despised,
denied justice and peace by the powerful ones. Amen.**

A Prayer for Relaxation

One: When we are controlled by time limits and appointments,

All: slow us down, O God, enable us to stop and take time to smell the roses.

One: When demands of friendship and relationships are intense,

All: slow us down, O God, give us the time we need to linger with our friends, to listen and to laugh with them.

One: When the news from our newspaper and television is of violence, fear and terror,

All: slow us down, O God, enable us to see the good news within the bad, and the hint of hope in the darkness.

One: When our faith life is troubled and confusing,

All: slow us down, O God, empower us to take the necessary time for prayer, reflection, and the time to simply "be."

Time of reflection…

Assurance of Peace

One: Peace, your own peace, such as the world cannot give, is what we seek, O God;

All: peace in our world, peace in our homes, peace in our own hearts.

One: Put your troubled hearts at rest, banish your fears and know God's peace, which passes all understanding.

All: Thanks be to God! Amen.

Offering Prayer

One: Our loyalty to you, O God, is reflected in our offering.

All: Serving you, we will rejoice in worship.
Serving you, we will care for the friendless.
Serving you, we will confront the evil ones.

One: Our love for God finds expression in serving God.

All: Amen.

Commissioning

One: Go from here as disciples of Jesus Christ.

All: Christ's words inspire us;
Christ's actions encourage us;
Christ's insight clarifies for us;
Christ's love enfolds us;
Christ's Spirit defines us.

Sunday between August 7 & 13 inclusive

Proper 14 [19]

Lectionary Readings

Genesis 37:1-4, 12-28
Psalm 105:1-6, 6-22, 45b
or
1 Kings 19:9-18
Psalm 85:8-13

Romans 10:5-15
Matthew 14:22-33

Call to Worship

One: Great Giver of Dreams, be with us on this Sunday morning;
All: allow our prayers and praise to soar, our imaginations to venture.
One: Inspirer of Faith, be with us on this Sunday morning;
All: encourage us to hear the Word, and make the Word live in our actions.
One: Just and Wonderful Friend, be with us on this Sunday morning;
All: come with us to comfort those who have suffered loss, and give the oppressed hope.
One: Eternal One, be with us on this Sunday morning,
All: putting time in its place, pointing us towards a glory that never ends.

Opening Prayer

One: The first day of the week, the day of new beginnings;
All: God, who created Sunday, we praise you.
One: The day of rest and reflection, the day to pause from the routine of life;
All: God, who made the Sabbath holy, we worship you.
One: The remembrance day of resurrection, the day of Jesus risen from the dead;

All: **God, who has given us new life in the risen Christ, we adore you.**
One: The day of certainty that our world is your world;
All: **God, present, active, at the heart of all our days, we thank you. Amen.**

Prayer of Confession

One: When we are tempted to give in to the popular but unjust way,
All: **steadfast God, forgive us.**
One: When we are tempted to leave the tough but necessary support to others,
All: **God of never-ending compassion, forgive us.**
One: When the powerful ones pressure us to compromise our principles,
All: **God, friend of the oppressed, forgive us.**
One: When we are tempted to ignore the needs of the community of faith,
All: **God, source and inspiration of the Church, forgive us.**
Time of reflection…

Words of Assurance

One: God does not remain apart from you; God is involved.
All: **You will enter into our struggle of heart and mind, O God; you will enable us to stand firm, and take the principled path.**
One: In a new sense of commitment, in a renewed sense of the Holy Spirit for you and with you, you have nothing to fear!
All: **Our faith is strengthened; we are ready for new patterns of service.**
One: Pardon and peace are yours.
All: **Thanks be to God! Amen.**

Offering Prayer

One: God's support of us is constant and reliable; God will never let us down!
All: **In Jesus, we have the assurance that he was there for those who needed him.**
One: These offerings are for the work of God in this faith community and far beyond.
All: **They will provide support, learning, challenge, confidence, and the opportunity of new ways.**

One: God will bless them, and bless us as we share in the work these gifts make possible.

All: To God be the glory! Amen.

Commissioning

One: "How beautiful are the feet of those who bring the Good News," writes Paul.

All: How strong are the hands of those who have the skills to build and repair, and are ready to use them.
How insightful are the eyes of those who see the lonely and the neglected, and are ready to help them.
How faithful are the voices of those who are aware of poverty and injustice, and will not keep quiet.
How useful are the ears of those who hear the deepest concerns of the troubled, and stay with them.

Sunday between August 14 & 20 inclusive

Proper 15 [20]

Lectionary Readings
Genesis 45:1-15
Psalm 133
or
Isaiah 56:1, 6-8
Psalm 67

Romans 11:1-2a, 29-32
Matthew 15:(10-20), 21-28

Call to Worship (based on Psalm 133)

One: How wonderful it is for God's people to live together in harmony:
All: to gather for worship, to rejoice in thanksgiving.
One: How wonderful it is for God's people to live together in harmony:
All: to encourage each other to be good friends.
One: How wonderful it is for God's people to live together in harmony:
All: to work together to support the troubled, near and far away.
One: How wonderful it is for God's people to live together in harmony:
All: to have the promised blessing, life that never ends.

Opening Prayer

One: Rejoice! We come to give thanks for the abundant gifts God has provided.
All: God is gracious; God's wonders can be seen and experienced.
One: Rejoice! We come to praise God as God's people together.
All: God will receive our offering, and challenge us to work faithfully within this fellowship, and build up our fellow members.
One: Rejoice! We come to proclaim ourselves as followers of Jesus Christ.
All: Christ's example is clear for us; Christ's death challenges us; Christ's risen presence is eternal hope for us.

One: Rejoice! We come to envision Christ in the most unlikely places and people.

All: Our commitment is proved as we meet Christ in the unloved and suffering, and befriend them.

One: Rejoice!

All: Our hearts overflow with thanksgiving to you, our ever-present God. Amen.

A Prayer for Christian Commitment (Confession)

One: Many choices await us in the daily routine of life.

All: In the will to make faithful decisions, in our rejection of selfishness, may persistence be our watchword.

One: Many opportunities are open for us to use our gifts.

All: In our recognition of new talents, in the choice of fresh ventures, may we overcome our fear of failure.

One: Many ways are open for us to find fellowship.

All: In our willingness to worship together, in our common action for good, may we find satisfaction in a faithful routine.

One: Many forces of evil confront us as we search for the authentic way.

**All: In our readiness to speak out against cruelty and hatred,
in our work for the powerless ones, may we stay the course.**

Time of silence…

Words of Assurance

One: Know freedom from doubt, know new confidence, know that your Christian faith will strengthen you!

All: In Christ we are revived and renewed.

One: Pardon and peace are yours.

All: Thanks be to God. Amen.

Offering Prayer

One: We celebrate the ability to give for our fellowship, and to care for others.

All: Receive our gifts, O God, and bless them.
Give us joy in our giving,
satisfaction as we see our money go to work,
and a reminder of all you have given to us, in the life, death, and rising of Jesus. Amen.

Commissioning

One: Deepen our faith, O God:

All: deepen our understanding of your Word;
keep us open to the prompting of the Spirit;
broaden the scope of our compassionate acts;
inspire us to new endeavours in this faith community;
enable us to support the world-wide church.

Sunday between August 21 & 27 inclusive

Proper 16 [21]

Lectionary Readings

Exodus 1:8 – 2:10
Psalm 124
or
Isaiah 51:1-6
Psalm 138

Romans 12:1-8
Matthew 16:13-20

Call to Worship

One: The cloud-capped hills are silent evidence of God's power.
All: The color and variety of trees and flowers, bear witness to the Holy One.
One: The smile on a baby's face speaks of God's renewing miracle in humankind.
All: The knowing glance of an older person mirrors the wise, accepting God.
One: Praise and glory, honor and blessing, be to the God who has created us,
the God who has formed us as a community of faith,
the God whose love goes beyond the boundaries of time and space.
All: Let us worship God!

Opening Prayer

One: O God, you rejoice with us in the warmth and relaxation of summer, meet with us in worship this morning;
All: give us the peaceful space, which will allow us to reflect on your many gifts to us.
One: Meet with us in this our summer worship;
All: give us the openness, which will enable us to hear the appropriate word.

One: Meet with us as a fellowship of friends;
All: give us the courage to walk the hard road of Christian discipleship together.
One: Meet with us as members of the worldwide Christian family;
All: give us the willingness to share from our plenty with our needy brothers and sisters of other towns, cities, and nations.

Prayer of Confession

One: O God, you call us to be "rocks" like Peter, but often we are more like clay.
All: We make clear our principles, but then compromise and give in. Forgive us!
One: O God, you call us to be "rocks" like Peter, but often we are more like sand.
All: We know the words that need to be said, but words fail us at the crucial time. Forgive us!
One: O God, you call us to be "rocks" like Peter, but often we are like a loose pile of stones.
All: We try to go it on our own, although our strength lies in what we can accomplish with others. Forgive us!
One: O God, you call us to be "rocks" like Peter, but often we are cracked and fragmented.
All: We go in several directions at once when we need focus and a goal, like Jesus. Forgive us!

Time of reflection...

Words of Assurance

One: God of all our days, you are with us.
**All: You strengthen us as we receive insight into our failings;
you encourage us as we are ready to take a stand;
you bless us as we work joyfully with others;
you renew us as faith gets the upper hand.**
One: With God, peace and a fresh start are realities.
All: We rejoice in God's graciousness! Amen.

Offering Prayer

One: Living God, you sustain us with gifts which are life to us;
All: may these offered gifts be life to this community and to the wider church.
May they bring light to those in darkness,
and hope to the despairing and fearful.
One: The life of Jesus is seen in the use of these gifts;
All: the life to guide and direct us. Amen.

Commissioning

One: Go to the world. God will change your attitude and set you to work!
All: We go with minds open to receive new truth;
we go with spirits attuned to God's challenging Word;
we go with hearts moved to act with compassion;
we go as disciples ready to follow Jesus, who is the Way.
One: God goes with you!

Sunday between August 28 & September 3 inclusive

Proper 17 [22]

Lectionary Readings
Exodus 3:1-15
Psalm 105:1-6, 23-26, 45c
or
Jeremiah 15:15-21
Psalm 26:1-8

Romans 12:9-21
Matthew 16:21-28

Call to Worship

One: Give thanks to God, and be faithful!
All: God provided for the people of Israel in the midst of the desert.
One: Give thanks to God, and be faithful!
All: God stood with the prophets, when everyone was against them.
One: Give thanks to God, and be faithful!
All: God was with Jesus as wholeness was restored, and evil defeated.
One: Give thanks to God, and be faithful!
All: God stands with us in the celebrations, and the testing times of life, and will not quit when time ends.

Opening Prayer

One: Come with Jesus, carry your cross.
All: We will put self on one side and value others.
One: Come with Jesus, carry your cross.
All: Success in the eyes of the world is not what God wants.
One: Come with Jesus, carry your cross,
All: Though we are burdened, others will find freedom.
One: Come with Jesus, carry your cross,
All: The act of carrying brings light to the dark places.
One: Come with Jesus, carry your cross.

All: For in harmony with Jesus, the way of life is clear. Amen.

Prayer for Thankful Hearts

One: God, you have given us life, and the nourishment, the laughter, and the friendship through which we enjoy life.

All: When we have neglected our thanksgiving for your many blessings, forgive us.

One: God, you have given us the community, the challenge, and the will to make our faith life effective.

All: When we have been slow to show our thanksgiving within this faith community, forgive us.

One: God, you have given us a life's journey to take, and the resources to undertake that journey with confidence and trust.

All: When we have forgotten your Way, or forgotten to thank you in our journeying, forgive us.

One: God, you have given us the person of Jesus Christ to follow, and the courage to walk in his footsteps.

All: When our fear has held us back, and when our thanksgiving has been half-hearted, forgive us.

Time of reflection...

Words of Assurance

One: It is as we reflect on our life in the light of Jesus Christ,

All: we recognize our need for a new way and a fresh start.

One: It is as we determine to make changes in our style of life,

All: we receive confidence as people whom God loves.

One: It is as we recognize our common strength in this community of faith,

All: we go forward joyfully, knowing that God's pardon and peace have been gracefully received. Amen.

Offering Prayer

One: God will provide for us in good times and in bad;

All: we can trust God.

One: God will use us to provide for others, near and far, in good times and in bad;

All: through our offerings, others will trust God.

One: We give joyfully, and we give generously, for we are about holy work.

All: God will bless us in our giving; God will bless those touched by our gifts. Amen.

Commissioning (Romans 9:12-21, adapted)

One: Love sincerely; hold fast to what is good!

All: We will confront the evil ones, but support each other; we will be zealous, ardent in spirit, and serve God faithfully.

One: Love genuinely; hold fast to what is good!

All: We will rejoice in hope, be patient in suffering, and persevere in prayer; we will give to the needs of this faith community, but also give to the oppressed in different cities and nations.

One: Love wholeheartedly; hold fast to what is good!

All: We will "turn the other cheek," celebrate with the joyful, and stand with the sorrowing; practice harmony and humility, and never seek to get revenge.

One: Love deeply; hold fast to what is good!

All: It is hard to be compassionate to those who are our enemies; to help them rather than harm them. But that is what we will be about – overcoming evil with good.

Sunday between September 4 & 10 inclusive

Proper 18 [23]

Lectionary Readings

Exodus 12:1-24
Psalm 149
or
Ezekiel 33:7-11
Psalm 119:33-40

Romans 13:8-14
Matthew 18:15-20

Call to Worship

One: Even with a congregation of two or three,
All: you will be present with us, O God.
One: Even with our record of ignoring and neglect,
All: you will be present with us, O God.
One: Even with our questions and doubts,
All: you will be present with us, O God.
One: Even as we risk and adventure,
All: you will be present with us, O God.
One: Even when our world is turned upside down,
All: you will be present with us, O God.
We will worship the Ever-Present God.

Opening Prayer

One: Out of grace beyond imagining, God created us;
All: we rejoice that we can bring thanksgiving and praise to God.
One: With the needs of family, friends, and the vulnerable, God has challenged us;
All: we rejoice that we can call on God to help us meet those needs.
One: Through the Bible, through the words of leaders, prophets, and Jesus Christ, God has spoken to us;

All: we rejoice that God's Word is an inspiration and a guide to us.

One: In the midst of this community of faith, God has given us fellowship;

All: we rejoice in the friendships and the common acts of service, which are ours.

One: In a world where inequality reigns, and the powerless struggle, God calls us to act;

All: we rejoice in the privilege to serve, as Christ has served before us. Amen.

Prayer of Confession

One: When we are tempted to evade the accusations of others,

All: give us the courage to face the issues directly.

One: When we are tempted to take advantage of our power or position,

All: give us the courage to walk in the shoes of the powerless.

One: When we are tempted to compromise the truth,

All: give us the courage to stand for what we know to be right.

One: When we are tempted to ignore the demands of our Christian faith,

All: give us the courage of Jesus, who was faithful all the way to the Cross.

Time of reflection...

Words of Assurance

One: As we confess our sins to God, we convince one another of our opportunity to begin again;

All: as we walk confidently in a new direction, pardon and peace are ours.

One: Believe deep in your hearts that God accepts and forgives you.

All: We believe in God's acceptance and forgiveness through Christ. Thanks be to God! Amen.

Offering Prayer

One: We do not ask, O God, that through our gifts all will be made perfect.

All: We ask that through our gifts
comfort will be experienced,
friendship will blossom,
neighbours will be discovered,
and those whose names we will never know will find courage and hope.
We pray in the name of God's Sharing One, Jesus. Amen.

Commissioning

One: Into this time of Pentecost, the Holy Spirit will breathe change.

All: Into our family circle, O God, breathe a sense of acceptance.
Into our friendship circle, O God, breathe a willingness to be open.
Into our community of faith, O God, breathe a sense of your insightful Word.
Into our troubled world, O God, breathe the intention of peace.
Into the depths of our being, O God, breathe the reality of your limitless love.

Sunday between September 11 & 17 inclusive

Proper 19 [24]

Lectionary Readings
Exodus 14:19-31
Psalm 114 or Exodus 15:1b-11, 20-21
or
Genesis 50:15-21
Psalm 103:(1-7), 8-13

Romans 14:1-12
Matthew 18:21-35

Call to Worship

One: God's call comes clearly to us;
All: we will listen and respond.
One: God's support is there for us
in times of stress and peril;
**All: we will know a secure peace,
and return our thanks to God.**
One: God's challenge is before us;
**All: God will give us the courage
to meet the challenge, in the Way of Jesus Christ.**

Opening Prayer

One: Loving God, you sustain us when our world crumbles.
You are there for us when other supports fall away.
**All: Enable us to search out the unseen glory and strength
that will keep us secure when the hard times come home to us.**
One: Even though we feel like giving up,
even though the way ahead seems without hope,
you, O God, are "the rock" that will not move.

All: In our darkness, you are light;
in our uncertainty, you are always the same;
in our despair, you are simply hope;
in our fear, you will not give in;
and you put us back on the faithful path that Jesus pioneered.
Yes, you are there for us! Amen.

A Prayer of Forgiveness

One: You remind us, O God, just how hard it is to forgive,

All: when a friend or a well-loved family member has betrayed our trust.

One: You remind us, O God, just how hard it is to forgive,

All: when harsh words have been said that cannot be taken back.

One: You remind us, O God, just how hard it is to forgive,

All: when a promise of support, challenge, or care has been broken.

One: You remind us, O God, just how hard it is to forgive,

All: when harm is done to children or to the powerless ones.

Time of reflection…

Words of Assurance

One: You know, O God, the difficulty of "from the heart" forgiveness when we have been hurt badly, or one of your children has been hurt.

All: But you call us to speak words that bring peace and reconciliation, and let our actions match our words.

One: "Lord if someone sins against me, how often should I forgive? Seven times?"

All: Jesus said to him, "Not seven times, seventy-seven times"

Offering Prayer

One: These are our purposeful gifts, O God;
they are given so that the faith community may be strengthened.

All: Through them, the lonely will be befriended;
with them, the suffering will be supported;
through them, the bereaved will be comforted;
with them, the cause of justice will be addressed,

One: and glory will be given to your name.

All: Praise to the gracious God! Amen.

Commissioning

One: We seek the values of your kingdom as we leave this church:

All: forgiveness, when the hurt deserves vengeance,
affirmation, when the first step has been a small one,
friendship, when the approach has been tentative,
Christian love, when there has been no effort to understand.

One: Christ lived out nothing less;

All: and we are his followers!

Sunday between September 18 & 24 inclusive

Proper 20 [25]

Lectionary Readings
Exodus 16:2-15
Psalm 105:1-6, 37-45
or
Jonah 3:10 – 4:11
Psalm 145:1-8

Philippians 1:21-30
Matthew 20:1-16

Call to Worship (Inspired by Psalm 105)

One: Give thanks to the Holy One!
All: God is great, and is the source of all good.
One: Bring praise to the Holy One!
All: Spread the word about all God has done.
One: Be glad that you belong to the Most High God!
All: God's encouragement is continually there for God's faithful people.
One: God's wisdom is available for all nations and people;
All: God's covenant holds fast for a thousand generations.

Opening Prayer

One: You call us to a generous way of being, O God.
All: When our praise and prayer come from the heart, you cheer us on.
One: You call us to a generous form of friendship, O God.
All: When we listen carefully and encourage with sensitivity, your presence is felt.
One: You call us to a generous spirit as we work, O God.
All: When we help out carefully, and share our rewards sacrificially, your Word is heeded.

One: You call us to look at the generosity of Jesus, O God.
All: And as we look up at the cross, we know how far generosity can go. Amen.

Prayer of Confession

One: You give us all we need for the life that is good, Living God;
All: when we hoard selfishly, and refuse to acknowledge the needs of others, forgive us!
One: You give us all we need for the faith life that is good, Living God;
All: when we take our Christian community for granted,
when we ignore the Bible teachings, forgive us!
One: You give us all we need for the prayer life that is good, Living God;
All: when we will not spare time for reflection, and refuse the ways that lead to peace, forgive us!
One: You give us all we need for the life that is good, Living God;
All: when we share generously, praise lavishly, and give without the thought of getting, you cheer us on, Loving God.
Time of reflection…

Words of Assurance

One: Loving God, your people are ready to change and experience forgiveness.
All: Make us as good at giving as getting;
as anxious about the needs of others as our own needs;
as conscious of your Word to us as the words that come at us from radio, TV, and popular magazines;
as certain that we can experience forgiveness as we are ready to forgive.
One: As you realize your own shortcomings and believe in your many gifts, God opens up the way for a new start. Know peace!
All: Thanks be to God. Amen.

Offering Prayer

One: Why is it that you offer your gifts to God?
**All: We give, not because it is our duty,
but because of God's unlimited generosity to us.
We give not just to help those in our fellowship or neighbourhood who are needy,
but to bring hope to persons unknown to us.
We give not just these gifts of money, but our best talents and abilities, and a priority of time, to be used in God's service.**
One: We give, O Loving God, always mindful of
your measureless gift in Jesus Christ. Amen.

Commissioning

One: The God whose love is unbounded, and whose generosity is limitless, goes with you on your way.
**All: God, a friend who knows the depth of our feeling,
the full extent of our fearing.
God, an encourager who knows the scope of our talent,
and the store of energy we can summon.
God, a challenger who asks the significant questions,
and will not be put off by superficial answers.
God, a loved one with us in the tough times of life,
yet celebrating with us when all goes well.
God goes with us; God will never leave us.**

Sunday between September 25 & October 1 inclusive

Proper 21 [26]

Lectionary Readings

Exodus 17:1-7
Psalm 78:1-4, 12-16
or
Ezekiel 18:1-4, 25-32
Psalm 25:1-9

Philippians: 2:1-13
Matthew 21:23-32

Call to Worship

One: Come to the water's edge!
All: Love is gently flowing, it's God's wondrous stream;
One: senses are on fire, touching thought and dream,
All: love is gently flowing, joy is unrestrained,
One: hearts are bursting, spirits thirsting,
All: we and God are one, in the river of time.

Opening Prayer

One: You are our friend, O God, and we rejoice.
All: As a friend, you invite us into your special place, and make us welcome.
One: You are our friend, O God, and we are thankful.
All: As a friend, you make us feel at home with your other friends; you encourage fellowship.
One: You are our friend, O God, and we celebrate.
All: As a friend, you laugh and smile with us, and encourage us when we feel low.
One: You are our friend, O God, and we praise you.
All: As our Eternal Friend, your grace overwhelms us and your promises in time, and beyond time leave us breathless. Amen.

Prayer of Testing (Confession)

One: Your unconditional love, the love we have seen in Jesus Christ, tests us, O God.

All: It tests us when suffering is least deserved and least expected. It tests us when the question is posed, "Why that person?" or "Why me?"

One: Your unconditional, unselfish love is tested, O God, when trouble comes to a life that has been worthy or selfless.

All: Your unselfish love is tested, O God, when from our family or faith community comes a cry for help.

One: Your unselfish love is tested, O God, when we are the ones in control, the ones with the power, the ones who can take advantage.

Time of reflection...

One: In our moments of testing be with us, O God;

All: lift our eyes from ourselves and from our faith community, to the cross.

Through the endurance of Jesus, through the cruel tragedy, through the saving grace, show us what can be achieved. Amen.

Words of Assurance

One: In the light of the self-giving, generous, and compassionate love of Jesus, your lives are revealed as shadowed and flawed.

All: We resolve to walk the Way of Christ.

One: This is the way in which God's pardon and peace are experienced; your sins are history!

All: Thanks be to God! Amen.

Offering Prayer

One: You are the means, O God, through which our small offerings become powerful gifts.

All: Bless those who receive, that they may know reassurance and healing, freedom and inspiration, friendship and renewed hope.

One: May they return thanks to you.

All: We pray in Jesus' name. Amen.

Commissioning

One: Grant to us, O God, the ability to
see things from your perspective.

All: To see the riches in humor and endurance of those poor in this world's goods;
to see the freedom of those persecuted for their beliefs;
to see the spiritual health of those who are suffering and at risk;
to see the wealth of friendship among those who find it difficult to travel freely;
to see the vitality of those who are going through the valley of the shadow.

Sunday between October 2 & 8 inclusive

Proper 22 [27]

Lectionary Readings
Exodus 20:1-4, 7-9, 12-20
Psalm 19
or
Isaiah 5:1-7
Psalm 80:7-15

Philippians 3:4b-14
Matthew 21:33-46

Call to Worship

One: We come to remember Jesus, the faithful one.
All: "The stone that the builders rejected has become the cornerstone."
One: We come with praise for Jesus, the compassionate one.
All: "The stone that the builders rejected has become the cornerstone."
One: We come to listen to Jesus, the teacher.
All: "The stone that the builders rejected has become the cornerstone."
One: We come to follow Jesus, the crucified and risen one.
All: "The stone that the builders rejected has become the cornerstone."

Opening Prayer

One: Sustaining God, be with us!
All: Without you we are nothing; with you we find strength for each day.
One: Feeling God, be with us!
All: With your confidence we can break with the past, and find joy in facing new challenges.
One: God of the Church, be with us!
All: In your Spirit, fellowship becomes a reality and worship is heartfelt.
One: God of Jesus, the Christ, be with us!

All: **In the Christian Scriptures, the example of Jesus leads us on, and his risen presence strengthens us. Amen.**

Prayer of Confession

One: As we enjoy our comfortable existence and lifestyle,
All: **it is easy to reject those who speak of sharing and sacrifice.**
One: As we are at home, in our traditional modes of worship and service,
All: **it is easy to reject those who call us to try some different approaches.**
One: As we have built up over the years a set of values and principles,
All: **it is easy to reject those who question the same values and principles.**
One: As we have come to see Jesus from our own Christian faith perspective,
All: **it is easy to reject those who see Jesus Christ differently.**

Time of reflection…

Words of Assurance

One: Your acceptance of us, O God, is so all-embracing,
so regardless of time or space, that it takes our breath away;
All: **we will respond to your acceptance of us,**
by a review of those who we find difficult to accept.
One: In a change of attitude, in a change of heart,
God's peace will be there.
All: **Thanks be to God! Amen.**

Offering Prayer

One: O God, may these gifts be used as Jesus would have used them:
All: **to speak out for justice in our neighbourhood,**
to encourage compassion among those who are distressed,
to foster friendship within our faith community,
to give thanks and praise to you, Loving God,
for all your graceful gifts.
One: You will be blessed as this money goes to work. Amen.

Commissioning

One: May God give us eyes to see the Christ in those around us.

All: Give us insight to feel the loneliness of the one who says, "everything's fine;"
give us courage to speak out for the person who is being ignored;
give us the willingness to stand beside those who suffer for Christian principles;
give us confidence to listen carefully to those who express their fears;
give us determination to work for justice with the person who confronts the powerful.

One: God will open your eyes; you will see.

All: Thanks be to God.

Sunday between October 9 & 15 inclusive

Proper 23 [28]

Lectionary Readings

Exodus 32:1-14
Psalm 106:1-6, 19-23
or
Isaiah 25:1-9
Psalm 23

Philippians 4:1-9
Matthew 22:1-14

Call to Worship

One: You invite us to worship, O God, and we rejoice!
All: We are able to leave the anxieties of our daily lives behind.
One: You invite us to worship, O God, and we give thanks!
All: We realize the full extent of your wonderful gifts.
One: You invite us to worship, O God, and we remember!
All: We are aware of your love, so graciously shown in Jesus Christ.
One: You invite us to worship, O God, and we respond!
All: We are ready to act compassionately and justly, in Christ's name.

Opening Prayer

One: O God, your steadfast love is always there for us;
All: there in times of joy, there when the testing times come.
One: O God, your steadfast love is always there for us;
All: there when apathy grips us, there when enthusiasm is ours.
One: O God, your steadfast love is always there for us;
All: there in our solitary moments, there when we share in faith community.
One: O God, your steadfast love is always there for us;
All: there as we stay in familiar territory, there as we venture and risk. Your love never leaves us! Amen.

Prayer of Confession

One: So many things are obstacles to our faithfulness, O God;

All: we are locked into a comfortable and routine existence; it is hard to change.

One: So much keeps us in the familiar rut, O God;

All: the invitation comes to try out new skills, to risk faithfully, but we turn it down.

One: So much distracts us from committing to the faith community, O God;

All: the needs of family and friends, the obligation to social groups, take up our time.

One: So many values conflict with our Christian values, O God;

All: the subtle pressure to go with the latest trend, the pressure to ignore the pain of humankind's global family.

Time of reflection...

Words of Assurance

One: The call has come for you to leave your comfortable distractions, and to focus on the values of God's realm;

All: we will carefully review our priorities and values; we will seek out the Way of Christ and follow it.

One: If your commitment is strong, there is nothing you cannot achieve. You will experience God's peace as you venture out.

All: Thanks be to God! Amen.

Offering Prayer

One: These are the gifts of God's people. God will bless their use.

**All: They will be blessed as the Gospel is faithfully proclaimed;
they will be blessed as the suffering are supported,
and the bereaved are comforted;
they will be blessed as the faith community is nurtured;
they will be blessed as the hungry receive food,
and the disadvantaged receive job training;
they will be blessed as we are willing to take responsibility
for their effectiveness.**

One: There are no limits to God's blessing!

All: God be praised! Amen.

Commissioning (Philippians 4)

One: "Rejoice in the Lord always,
I will say it again, 'Rejoice!'"

**All: We will rejoice with kind thoughts, and gentle acts;
we will rejoice as we pray hopefully, and reflect carefully;
we will rejoice as we hold the example of the saints before us;
we will rejoice when life is wonderful, and when life is a trial.**

One: And the peace of God, which surpasses all understanding, will guard your hearts and minds in Christ Jesus.

Sunday between October 16 & 22 inclusive

Proper 24 [29]

Lectionary Readings
Exodus 33:12-23
Psalm 99
or
Isaiah 45:1-7
Psalm 96:1-9, (10-13)

1 Thessalonians 1:1-10
Matthew 22:15-22

Call to Worship

One: The seventh day, Sunday, is a blessing for us, O God:
All: a day when most can rest and relax, and forget the demands of the workplace.
One: The seventh day, Sunday, is a blessing for us, O God:
All: a day when we can focus on spiritual things, and reflect and pray.
One: The seventh day, Sunday, is a blessing for us, O God:
All: a day when we can gather for worship, and share in the life of the faith community.
One: the seventh day, Sunday is a blessing for us, O God:
All: a day when we remember Jesus Christ, and glory in his rising from death.

Opening Prayer

One: You have promised to stay with us, O God;
All: when we rejoice and celebrate, you are there.
One: You have promised never to leave us, O God;
All: when we go our selfish way, you are there.
One: You have promised to remain faithful, O God,
All: and in Jesus Christ, your faithfulness is proved.

One: You have promised to always be with us,
All: and in time, and beyond time, you are there. Amen.

Prayer of Confession

One: It is sometimes difficult to keep the balance
between loyalty to the government, and loyalty to Christian principles.
All: We will reflect carefully on the issues, and keep the faith.
One: It is sometimes difficult to keep the balance
between loyalty to a friend and loyalty to the truth.
All: We will talk over our concerns, but will go the honest way.
One: It is sometimes difficult to keep the balance between the demands of family and demands outside the home.
All: We will faithfully consider our priorities, and listen to those closest to us.
One: It is sometimes difficult to keep the balance between loyalty to the bible stories we know and love, and new insights into the Word.
All: We will honor the tradition we have received, but be ready for new ventures.

Time of reflection…

Words of Assurance

One: God does not promise us the ease of clear decisions,
nor give us easy answers. God calls us to use our powers
of reasoning and judgement.
All: We will wrestle with our challenges; we will use our faith resources; we will not take the easy way out!
One: And God will bless your endeavors and grant you peace.
All: Thanks be to God! Amen.

Offering Prayer

One: Not our money alone, do we offer, O God.

All: Money is a universal way of helping, but money only goes so far.

One: Not our time alone, do we offer, O God.

All: Time is a precious commodity, but time is not enough.

One: Not our talent alone, do we offer, O God.

All: Talent is a way of giving personal gifts, but our abilities are limited.

One: But combine money, time, and talent, and you have a worthy offering;

All: this is what we do offer to you, our God, for blessing;
all will be carefully used in your service. Amen.

Commissioning

One: God will go with you every step of the way!
God's energy to invigorate you,
God's judgement to direct you,
God's Word to instruct you,
God's peace to enfold you,
God's love in Jesus Christ to secure you.

All: We go from this church refreshed,
and ready for God's work.

Sunday between October 23 & 29 inclusive

Proper 25 [30]

Lectionary Readings
Deuteronomy 34:1-12
Psalm 90:1-6, 13-17
or
Leviticus 19:1-2, 15-18
Psalm 1

1 Thessalonians 2:1-8
Matthew 22:34-46

Call to Worship (inspired by Psalm 90)

One From generation to generation, you are our God;
All: we praise and worship you!
One: Creator of our world, life force of every human being;
All: we praise and worship you!
One: Author of time, yet above and beyond all time;
All: we praise and worship you!
One: Steadfast in your love, each new day;
All: we praise and worship you!

Opening Prayer

One: With our lips we praise you, O God;
All: lips that speak of your awesome creation, and the wonder of your love.
One: With our minds we praise you, God;
All: minds to understand the depth of your compassion, and to work out your way of justice and mercy.
One: With our hearts we praise you, O God;
All: hearts to feel the generosity of your beloved one, Jesus, and to respond with faithful discipleship. Amen.

Prayer of Confession

One: Your commandment is clear to us, O God, and we will love you alone;
All: but there are other gods who claim our attention:
the god of getting and spending, the god of ease and comfort, the god of pride.
One: Your commandment is clear to us, O God, that we love our neighbour;
All: but we need to consider, "who is your neighbor?" The family next door? The needy persons of our community? The starving and despairing of this small planet?
One: Your commandment is clear to us, O God, that we love ourselves;
All: but we find it difficult to believe in ourselves, we doubt our talents and abilities, we compare ourselves unfavorably to our friends, we hold back from ventures.
Time of reflection…

Words of Assurance

One: We believe in you, O God, and you believe in us,
and so we go forward confidently.
All: We will put the other gods in their place;
we will serve our most needy neighbors;
we will identify and use the talents you have given us.
One: On your new path, God goes with you.
God's peace is yours!
All: Thanks be to God! Amen.

Offering Prayer

One: You bless us in our offering, O God;
you bless the worship and work our gifts make possible.

All: You bless our understanding of the Word;
you bless the fellowship we enjoy in this church;
you bless our links with other faith groups;
you bless the Christian witness we make day by day;
you bless our stand with the powerless;
you bless our work for peace in a troubled world.

One: You bless our gifts, for they have the Spirit of Jesus within them.

All: Amen.

Commissioning

One: The love of God goes with us as we leave this community of friends:

All: a love with which to strengthen one another,
a love to hold us secure in the turmoil of life,
a love that will allow us to risk,
a love to dispel the darkness,
a love to cast out fear,
a love to share, widely, generously,
a love that goes beyond limits of time or space,

One: a love we have known in Jesus Christ.

Sunday between October 30 & November 5 inclusive

Proper 26 [31]

Lectionary Readings
Joshua 3:7-17
Psalm 107:1-7, 33-37
or
Micah 3:5-12
Psalm 43

1 Thessalonians 2:9-13
Matthew 23:1-12

Call to Worship

One: May your Spirit fill our fellowship, Loving God,
All: and give us minds ready to appreciate your word.
One: May your Spirit fill our fellowship, Compassionate God,
All: and give us hearts responsive to the distressed.
One: May your Spirit fill our fellowship, Just God,
All: and give us a willingness to stand with the powerless.
One: May your Spirit fill our fellowship, Awe-inspiring God,
All: and keep us open and receptive to your leading.

Opening Prayer

One: Good News touches us as we worship this morning;
All: the limits we place on ourselves are gone.
One: Good News enlivens us as we worship this morning;
All: the limits we have placed on our faith community are broken.
One: Good News liberates us as we worship this morning;
All: the limits we have placed on our troubled world, to know harmony, are shattered.
One: Good News enfolds us as we worship this morning;

All: **for in Jesus Christ, you have spoken and acted, O God,**
and the limits are swept away. Amen.

Prayer of Affirmation (Confession)

One: The humility of Elijah is in the Hebrew Scriptures for us,
All: **and we understand that sometimes we hit the lowest point**
before hearing God's "still small voice."
One: The humility of Mary is in the Christian Scriptures for us,
All: **and we learn that an unexpected turn in a life's journey**
is not accepted without struggle.
One: The humility of Peter is in the Christian Scriptures for us,
All: **and it is clear that we can betray what is crucial to us**
before we see the truth.
One: The humility of Saul is in the Christian Scriptures for us,
All: **and we realize that our faith can become dynamic**
when the light dawns.
Time of reflection…

Words of Assurance

One: We find it easy to rely on appearances – to talk big but think small;
but you, O God, cut us down to size; you humble us.
All: **We will be alert for hypocrisy;**
we will practice what we preach;
we will see through the impressive façade;
we will seek out the way of true humility;
One: and God's pardon will be there for you.
All: **Thanks be to God! Amen.**

Offering Prayer

One: There is nothing ordinary about these gifts!

All: Through understanding, these gifts will banish fear;
through a comforting presence, these gifts will banish sadness;
through mission beyond this community, these gifts will touch persons needy but unknown;
through your Spirit, O God, these gifts will bring light to the dark places.
There is nothing ordinary about these gifts! Amen.

Commissioning

One: You have heard the Gospel challenge.
Go back into the world.

All: We will go into the world, open to new ideas and truth;
we will go into the world, ready to expose the hypocrites;
we will go into the world, ready to act humbly;
we will go into the world as followers of Jesus, whose insight clarifies and enlightens.

One: God goes with you!

Sunday between November 6 & 12 inclusive

Proper 27 [32]

Lectionary Readings

Joshua 24:1-3a, 14-25
Psalm 78:1-7
or
Wisdom of Solomon 6:12-16 or Amos 5:18-24
Wisdom of Solomon 6:17-20 or Psalm 70

1 Thessalonians 4:13-18
Matthew 25:1-13

Call to Worship

One: Are you ready for worship?
All: We have prayed that God will bless our time together.
We are ready!
One: Are you ready for worship?
All: Our church friends are with us, and they care for us.
We are ready!
One: Are you ready for worship?
All: We look forward to our part in the praise and the singing.
We are ready!
One: Are you ready for worship?
All: The stories of Jesus await us, the Holy Spirit will
send us out enthused.
We are ready!

Opening Prayer

One: You have been with us in the glory days of summer, O God;
All: you are with us as the nights draw in, and the cooler days are here.
One: You are with us in the carefree happy moments, O God;
All: you are with us when the darkness threatens, and times are hard.
One: You have been with us in the joyous company of family and friends;

All: you are with us when it seems no one is present,
and when we feel lonely.

One: You have been there for us when our faith was strong and vibrant;

All: you are there for us as we face our doubts,
and work through our concerns.

One: Sometimes you appear gone from us;

All: but you are always there for us, O Most Loving God! Amen.

Prayer of Confession

One: O God, we confess that the spirit of wonder has not always inspired our community.

All: Open our eyes, O God, to appreciate your mystery at the heart of creation.

One: The spirit of service has not always empowered our community.

All: Teach us, O God, to be sensitive to the needs of others,
and to meet them carefully.

One: The spirit of support has not always motivated our community.

All: Fill us, O God, with the desire to strengthen and uphold one another.

One: The spirit of sacrifice has not always marked our community.

All: Turn our faces to the cross, O God, that we may understand what it takes to overcome evil.

Time of reflection…

Words of Assurance

One: We will not remain unmoved by the fresh insights God has given us;

All: we will move from understanding to repentance, and a desire to bring change.

One: And the life work of Jesus Christ makes clear that change is possible.

All: We will take heart from the joy, the restored freedom,
and the restored health, of those touched by Jesus.

One: And you will know the Peace of God.

All: God be praised! Amen.

Offering Prayer

One: The spirit of giving changes, O God, as you become our partner.

All: Our reluctance becomes generosity;
our vision of offering widens to encompass gifts, skills and talents;
our focus changes to include national and international needs.

One: Transform our giving, Loving God, in the Way of Jesus.

All: We pray in his name. Amen.

Commissioning

One: Your faith is strong; you are determined!

All: We will respond to God wholeheartedly.

One: You are prepared for discipleship; you will follow Jesus!

All: We will meet Christ in our needy friends and neighbors.

One: You will work together; you are one in fellowship!

All: We will participate with enthusiasm in the life of the faith community.

One: Your faith *is* strong, you *are* determined!

Sunday between November 13 & 19 inclusive

Proper 28 [33]

Lectionary Readings
Judges 4:1-7
Psalm 123
or
Zephaniah 1:7, 12-18
Psalm 90:1-8, (9-11), 12

1 Thessalonians 5:1-11
Matthew 25:14-30

Call to Worship

One: As the apprentice looks to his craftsperson,
All: so we look to you, O God.
One: As a child looks to her mother or father,
All: so we look to you, O God.
One: As the loved one looks to their cherished partner,
All: so we look to you, O God.
One: As the seeker looks to a wise, faithful one,
All: so we look to you, O God.
One: As Jesus looked to the one he called "Abba," Father,
All: so we look to you, O God.

Opening Prayer

One: Living God, you are always concerned for your people;
All: you gave the slaves in Egypt Moses, the leader, to inspire them.
One: Holy God, you sought salvation for your people;
All: you gave the people Deborah, the prophet, to bring them hope.
One: Loving God, you came through when all seemed lost for your people;
All: you proved your love in Jesus, who rose from the abyss of crucifixion.
One: Ever-present God, you are with your people still;

All: **you give us saints, courageous and unsung, to meet the challenge of the times; you will never leave us! Amen.**

Prayer of Confession

One: You call us to use the talents you have given, O God;

All: **when we deny their existence, alert us to the insight of friends and loved ones.**

One: You call us to use the talents you have given, O God;

All: **when we are afraid of what people will say, give us the confidence to risk.**

One: You call us to use the talents you have given, O God;

All: **when we would keep them to ourselves, open our eyes to the increasing circles of need.**

One: You call us to use the talents you have given, O God;

All: **when we hold back from a generous response, lift our eyes to Jesus and his cross.**

Time of reflection…

Words of Assurance

One: You will be our partner in adventure, as we use fresh gifts and talents, O God.

All: **In the joy of success, and in the hard place of failure, you will be there.**

One: We will find you in the encouragement of a companion; we will know you in the compassion of a stranger;

All: **and at the end of the day, you will be there, the source of affirmation and peace.**

One: Yes, renewed courage and peace will be yours.

All: **Thanks be to God! Amen.**

Offering Prayer

One: You call on us, O God, to appreciate and use the array of talents with which you have equipped us;

All: We will combine them with the time and the treasure that is ours, and use them in your service.

One: The power of the faith community is formidable, when time, talent, and treasure are used together for good;

All: the striving church, here and overseas, and the shadowed world, are crying out for these gifts of faith.

One: Living God, bless them! Amen.

Commissioning

One: Go from this church to bring the change that God whole-heartedly seeks.

All: We will search out our talents carefully;
we will use our abilities generously;
we will share our time graciously;
we will open our horizons adventurously;
we will comfort the suffering tenderly;
we will confront the powerful openly.

One: And the God who gave us Jesus will give you peace.

Reign of Christ Sunday – between November 20 & 26 inclusive

Proper 29 [34]

Lectionary Readings

Ezekiel 34:11-16, 20-24
Psalm 100
or
Ezekiel 34:11-16, 20-24
Psalm 95:1-7a

Ephesians 1:15-23
Matthew 25:31-46

Call to Worship

One: In our circle of uncertainty and hurry,
All: you, O God, are the fixed point of calm.
One: In our stretched moments of stress and emotion,
All: you, O God, are the settled feeling of peace.
One: In our well-worn routine of the everyday,
All: you, O God, are the flash of fresh inspiration.
One: In our ordinary and earthbound moments,
All: you, O God, are the Spirit that transforms through the holy.

A Prayer for the Reign of Christ

One: Come, O Risen Christ, and reign among us!
All: Our worship will be joyful, insightful, and free.
One: Come, O Risen Christ, and reign among us!
All: Our faith community will be enthusiastic, supportive, and ready to serve.
One: Come, O Risen Christ, and reign among us!
All: The downhearted will know hope, and the suffering, peace.
One: Come, O Risen Christ, and reign among us!
All: The faiths of the world will join hands, and fear will come to an end. Amen.

A Prayer of Longing and Confession

One: We long for Christ's reign on earth; we will know release from all that keeps us bound.

All: Where we lack freedom, O God, give us the courage to risk change.

One: We long for Christ's reign on earth; the poor and powerless will get a fair deal.

All: Where we lack generosity, O God, encourage us to share.

One: We long for Christ's reign on earth; the vulnerable ones will gain confidence.

All: Where we lack acceptance, O God, open our eyes to see the downtrodden.

One: We long for Christ's reign on earth; those held back and restricted will feel free.

All: When we lack a liberating attitude, O God, enable us to work in fresh ways.

One: We long for Christ's reign on earth; the faithful will be joyful and active in the community.

All: When we lack involvement, O God, open us up to new initiatives of compassion and community support.

Time of reflection…

Words of Assurance

One: Work patiently to bring closer the reign of Christ.

All: We will need new attitudes, fresh vision, and a change of heart.

One: God will grant you the strength – spiritual, emotional, and practical.

All: We are ready!

One: Pardon, peace, and a new determination are yours.

All: Thanks be to God! Amen.

Offering Prayer

One: These gifts will enable the face of Christ to be seen –
All: among the sick,
among the distressed,
among the fearful,
among the lonely,
among the depressed,
among those who lack confidence –
One: a compassionate, understanding, and friendly face.
All: Bless these offerings, for we bring them in Christ's name. Amen.

Commissioning

One: Go from here as those committed to bring Christ's reign closer.
All: We will be a challenge to the powerful;
we will be a support to the suffering;
we will be a word of hope to the despairing;
we will be a beacon of hope to the uncertain;
we will be an encouraging presence to the venturesome.
One: Go with confidence, go in peace!

All Saints Sunday

November 1 or the first Sunday in November

Lectionary Readings

Revelation 7:9-17
Psalm 34:1-10, 22
1 John 3:1-3
Matthew 5:1-12

Call to Worship

One: The saints call us to worship;
All: Martin Luther says, "remember your reformed tradition."
One: The saints call us to worship;
All: Patrick of Ireland reminds us, "you are about the task of mission."
One: The saints call us to worship;
All: Dietrich Bonhoeffer is clear, "you have to get involved in the struggle against evil powers."
One: The saints call us to worship;
All: Mother Theresa points out the dying and the despised, and tells us, "they are your responsibility."

Opening Prayer

One: We worship with all the saints of every age. They challenge us, they encourage us, they inspire us.
All: From the saints we learn that regular prayer nourishes the soul, and we remember Julian of Norwich.
One: We worship with all the saints;
All: From the saints we learn that the Christian life is nurtured in community, and we remember Francis of Assisi.
One: We worship with all the saints;
All: From the saints we learn that the Bible is worth suffering and sacrifice, and we remember William Tyndale.
One: We worship with all the saints;

All: From the saints we learn that the life of faith is a wonderful adventure, and we remember Paul.
We are blessed, for the saints are with us! Amen.

Prayer of Aspiration (Confession)

One: We notice the saints around us, O God; they have time for their friends and their family members.

All: We want to be like them.

One: We notice the saints around us, O God; they see a neighbor in need, and they are ready to meet that need.

All: We want to be like them.

One: We notice the saints around us, O God; they are aware of an injustice in the local community, or beyond this nation, and they find a way to bring change.

All: We want to be like them.

One: We notice the saints around us, O God; they have a strong faith, and are ready to nourish their faith in Christian community.

All: We want to be like them.

Time of reflection…

Words of Assurance

One: The qualities of sainthood are within your grasp: you have the ability, you have the opportunity.

All: We will strive to develop and to use those qualities of the saints that we dimly recognize.

One: When you are discouraged, remember that the saints of the ages struggled and suffered, but they won through gloriously.

All: We will keep the faith; we will stay the distance!

One: Peace, and a whole new attitude to life, will be yours!

All: Thanks be to God! Amen.

Offering Prayer

One: May your blessing, O God, bring these gifts to life;

All: new hope of healing, fresh ways of coping;
a chance to rest, a chance to work;
a way to live gracefully, a way to die peacefully.

One: May these gifts be used as Jesus Christ would use them.

All: Amen.

Commissioning

One: Go with the saints; go confidently!

All: We will pray faithfully;
we will care compassionately;
we will face the powerful joyfully;
we will share in community selflessly;
we will shed light in the dark places fearlessly;
we will proclaim Christ risen, gloriously!

One: And God will go with you as you leave the Church.

Thanksgiving Day

2nd Monday in October (Canada)/4th Thursday in November (USA)

Lectionary Readings
Deuteronomy 8:7-18
Psalm 65
2 Corinthians 9:6-15
Luke 17:11-19

Call to Worship

One: Creator and Sustainer of all humankind, source of the rains, author of the harvests,
All: we praise you as you have been praised from age to age.
One: Encourager of community, Spirit of careful sharing,
All: we thank you as you have been thanked from age to age.
One: Light-bringer to our darkness, inspirer of hope, whispering with the voice of conscience,
All: we worship you as you have been worshipped from age to age.
One: Awakener of the faith, provoker of the prophets, anointer of Jesus, your Chosen One,
All: we glorify you, as you have been glorified from age to age.

Prayer of Approach, a Thanksgiving Prayer

One: O God, we spread out our thanksgivings before you;
All: our thanksgiving for grain safely harvested, and for good food on our tables.
One: O God, we spread out our thanksgivings before you;
All: Our thanksgiving for family members who support us,
and for friends who stay with us.
One: O God, we spread out our thanksgivings before you;
All: our thanksgiving for times when we can walk, cycle, and play,
and times when we can relax at home.
One: O God, we spread out our thanksgivings before you;
All: for prayer and praise, for the scriptures, for our faith life as disciples of Christ.

One: As we spread our thanksgivings before you, we find the reason for our joyful celebration;
All: thank you, O Most Loving God! Amen.

A Prayer for Faithful Attitudes and Practices (Confession)

One: Looking at the star-filled heavens, faced with the beauty of flowers, the distinct taste of a peach or a tomato,
All: we hear your call to keep the air, the water, and the earth, clean for future generations.
One: Blessed by the presence of this gathered faith community,
All: we hear your call to support our fellow church members, in good times and in the hard times.
One: Surrounded by close family at the Thanksgiving table,
All: we will hear your call to remember our roots, and to affirm the worth of each family member.
One: Conscious of the variety of material goods, the friendships and relationships, and the good feelings we have to thank you for, O God,
All: we confess the ease with which we take your countless gifts for granted.

Time of reflection…

Words of Assurance

One: You hear our silent, heartfelt cry, O God,
All: for the world's needs, which we have seen as beyond our aid,
for our neighbour's needs, to which we have failed to respond,
for our own deep needs, which we have chosen to leave until tomorrow.
One: You are called to quietly face new realities;
you are called to small deeds of help and caring;
you are called to venture for change,
and as you progress, you will know peace.
All: Yes, God's peace will be ours; thanks be to God! Amen.

Offering Prayer

One: Your gifts are so overwhelming, so diverse, so graciously given, O God, that our hearts overflow with thanksgiving.

All: **What we offer in return is so small, so inadequate, so much a simple token;**
but we ask you to bless these gifts, and to bless their use, that those close at hand and those far away will feel your compassionate and hopeful presence.

One: Our offerings are presented in the name of Jesus, your perfect gift.

All: **Amen.**

Commissioning

One: Go from here with thanksgiving on your lips and in your hearts!

All: **As we return to greet our family we will give thanks;**
as we search out and help our neighbours, we will give thanks;
as we serve with others in the faith community, we will give thanks;
as we speak out on behalf of the powerless, we will give thanks;
as we praise our Most Loving God, we will give humble thanks.

One: Your thankful God goes with you!

Memorial/Remembrance/ Veterans' Sunday

Call to Worship

One: We remember those who fight against terror and fear-provokers,

All: and we ask God's presence with them and their families.

One: We remember those who in times past fought for freedom,

All: and we are thankful for their sacrifice.

One: We remember those who lost homes and loved ones,

All: and we are called to work for peace.

One: We remember those whose hearts are set on justice and reconciliation,

All: and we will support and encourage them.

One: We remember God's will for humankind is for all to live in a harmonious and compassionate way.

All: We remember that the Way of Jesus is a way of peace.

Opening Prayer

One: Holy One, you have come close to us in Jesus Christ; you know the whole range of human experience.
In times of joy and celebration, Loving God,

All: you laugh with us; you strengthen us as family and community.

One: In times of uncertainty and change, Loving God,

All: you are the Rooted One; you hold us fast when the storm strikes home.

One: In times of loss, when our most cherished dreams have been snatched away from us, Loving God,

All: You are the Enduring One, the voice of hope.

One: In times of warfare and terror, when it seems that calm will never return, Loving God,

All: you are the Peaceful One, the promise of shalom.

Prayer of Affirmation (Confession)

One: This is the way we honor the memory of men and women ready to lay down their lives.

All: We will not tolerate hatred, nor stand idly by when innocent men, women, and children are killed and injured.

One: This is the way we honor those who help refugees and political prisoners.

All: We will support them practically, and challenge corrupt governments to let the prisoners go free.

One: This is the way we put an end to the conflict that is a part of our own experience.

All: We will search out the source of our anger, and sense what it means to walk in another's shoes.

One: This is the way we will counter the influences of selfishness and fear that are known to us.

All: We will come humbly before you, our God, and take courage from the cross of Jesus the Christ.

Time of reflection…

Words of Assurance

One: Let us look carefully at those ways in which our own lifestyle denies our Christian discipleship.

All: We will take the time we need to come to fresh insights and understandings.

One: Let us look carefully at our patterns of community life and service.

All: We will take the time we need to plan a common life of faith.

One: Pardon and peace are yours.

All: Thanks be to God. Amen.

Offering Prayer

One: Remember that your gifts are blessed by the Holy One!

All: These gifts will promote a neighbourhood where harmony and tolerance are the norm;
these gifts will encourage a world where the developed nations share with those who have so little;

these gifts will bring the rejected and persecuted to a new land;
these gifts will be the means of healing and an end to fear;
these gifts will put the unsure on the road to confidence.

One: We offer them hopefully, O God.

All: Amen.

Commissioning

One: You leave this church with new thoughts and new intentions.

All: We leave deeply grateful for all who gave their lives,
and those scarred by war;
we leave as people realizing there is no shortcut to peace;
we leave as people committed to speak out against injustice;
we leave as people prepared to model reconciliation;
we leave as people ready to work toward understanding those of different races and faiths.

One: You go hopefully and joyfully, for God goes with you.

Thematic Index

H

I

S

T

Hebrew Scripture Index

New Testament Scripture Index

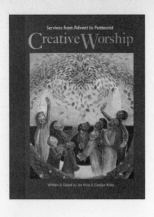

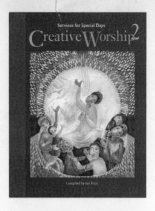